The
Caring
Child

T0386501

The Caring Child

Raising Empathetic and Emotionally Intelligent Children

Christine Fonseca

Routledge
Taylor & Francis Group

NEW YORK AND LONDON

First published in 2019 by Prufrock Press Inc.

Published 2021 by Routledge
605 Third Avenue, New York, NY 10017
2 Park Square, Milton Park, Abingdon, Oxon OX14 4RN

Routledge is an imprint of the Taylor & Francis Group, an informa business

Copyright © 2019 by Taylor & Francis Group

Cover design by Micah Benson and layout design by Allegra Denbo

Library of Congress catalog information currently on file with the publisher.

ISBN 13: 978-1-6182-1873-5 (pbk)

DOI: 10.4324/9781003238751

Dedication

Dedicated to today's children, part of a generation
that embraces tolerance in ways seldom before seen,
but for whom emotional strength is ever more elusive.
May this book guide you and the caring adults in your
lives to a more caring and compassionate world.

Table of Contents

Acknowledgments

WRITING for a living was not something I had initially planned to do. I had no idea that my first book in 2010 would lead to such a joyous vocation for me. None of it would be possible without the help and assistance of my family, friends, and community. Thanks for making another book possible.

To my partner, my husband, my soulmate—once again your support for my need to express myself in words is the reason I am able to write. You pick up the chores, run the errands, and make food anytime my ventures into the writing cave are too long. You listen to my endless prattling about whatever I am writing about without complaint. You're my strength when I am convinced I can't move forward, my consoler when I fall short of my goals, and my cheerleader when I soar. Thank you for being my partner on this crazy ride.

To my amazing children, Fabiana and Erika—you find ways into every book I write. You are my thought partners, my editors, my creative inspiration. Thank you for allowing me to pursue my crazy need to create without ever feeling like I have to sacrifice my relationships with you both.

The Caring Child

To Katy McDowall and the team at Prufrock Press—you have been my partner now for all of my nonfiction work. Your insight, belief in me, and ongoing commitment to publishing quality educational and parenting titles have made everything possible. I can never say thank you enough.

To my colleagues at Collaborative Learning Solutions: Jon, Gail, Kenny, Debbie, Mary Beth, Micki, Dean, and everyone else who makes the "daily grind" so worth it—the work we do every day inspires so much of my work as a writer, particularly with this book. Your collective dedication to disrupting the status quo in education and improving outcomes for kids is why I do this work. Thank you for letting me part of something that is so much more than a "job."

To my BFFs and cheer squad: Andrea, Stephanie, Jodi, and Chris—you are great friends, trusted confidants, and endless sources of inspiration. Although we have not spent near enough time together of late, your positive influence on my life and support for my creative work is never unnoticed. Thank you for your willingness to offer counsel, connections, and laughter.

To the hundreds of contributors around the world—you shared your thoughts and stories with me online, via e-mail, over Zoom, and in person, and shaped many of the strategies, role-play scenarios, and stories in the book. Thank you for your collective wisdom and engaging in my book research process so generously.

And finally, to the ever-inspiring writing community, bloggers, readers, and fans that continue to support and inspire my work— although I only know most of you through my online communities, our connections are real and feed my soul. You get me through the hard times, the moments I am convinced I will never write another word. Without your encouragement, willingness to share my work, and requests for more, I would not be blessed to continue down this author path. Thank you!

—*Christine Fonseca*

Author's Note

I am blessed to spend most hours of the day working with children or helping adults be more impactful in the work they do with children. As a result, I get a close view of the changing generations and the impact of world events on the daily lives of children. Over the last 5 years, I've noticed a significant shift—children are more tolerant but less emotionally flexible. Social-emotional learning (SEL) is receiving more and more attention, and yet children are less and less resilient. It's a paradox.

As I sifted through research to determine what was happening, it became clear to me that, although positive psychological constructs were having a generally positive impact, there were several unforeseen consequences. One of the more major of these is a growing belief that you "should" only feel happy all of the time; there is a feeling that sadder, more complex emotions are an indication that you aren't practicing positive psychological principles enough.

Add to this an increase in perceived pressure to perform from children, the impacts of technology on social development, and decreased self-esteem in the current generation of children, and it is not surprising that many experts feel that we are on the verge of a serious mental health crisis among our youth. An increase in trau-matic incidences, including adverse childhood experiences, commu-nity violence, and natural disasters, have only increased the assault on our children's social-emotional development, deepening the con-cerns around overall mental health.

Educators feel the shift, as do parents. Even our children talk about difficulties with resilience, increases in anxiety, and struggles with friendships. Schools, in an attempt to address the problem, have tried more positive approaches to discipline, with mixed results. Teachers express frustration with the changing social dynamics. Parents are concerned and struggling. Children are caught in the middle, unsure of how to respond to our current world.

This is the environment in which this book was born—a need to provide both parents and educators with additional tools to build empathy, raise resiliency, and better prepare our youth for an ever-changing world.

I hope that this book will challenge your thinking, explain the nature of empathy and compassion, and provide easy-to-use tools that can make a positive difference in your family and in schools. Many of the recommendations may sound simplistic. Many of the role-plays may feel awkward to replicate. I assure you that each and every strategy, suggestion, and practice has been used by me per-sonally, in my family, with clients, and in school settings. The recom-mendations are evidence-based and drawn from the latest research on the topics.

Take your time through the book. Refer to it whenever needed. My goal is to give you a resource that you can use over and over.

Happy reading!

Introduction

BROWSE through the local news on any given day and you will see headlines rife with stories about increased violence amongst our children: "Cyberbullying Causes Suicide in LGBTQ Youth," "Physical Aggression Among Middle School Girls Is on the Rise," "Adverse Childhood Experiences Cited as Cause of Mental Health Crisis Among Inner-City Children and Young Adults."

These aren't the only stories on the rise, however. There are other headlines, too. Ones that focus on hope: "High School Students Launch Sit-in Protest to Peacefully Force Attention on Discipline Process for Minorities," "Teens Go to Washington to Speak Out Against Gun Violence," "Elementary Girl Starts Fund to Raise Monies for Monument to Honor Native American War Heroes."

Although these are fictionalized headlines drawn from real stories over the past few years, the point is clear—we are living in dichotomous times in which children are both less compassionate and more tolerant, a time when our kids appear to be unable to handle life's awkward moments while also being the driving force behind significant positive change. The confusing nature of our current world makes it difficult to know precisely what we, as parents, need

1

DOI: 10.4324/9781003238751-1

to teach our children most. Do we need to do a better job of support-ing and nurturing the development of empathy and compassion? Or do we need to get out of the way and let the natural kindness of our children shine through, supporting our children's actions as they try to make a better world than we've left for them?

Both, I would say.

Our children are struggling. Although it is clear that this gen-eration of youth is more aware and tolerant of culture shifts, these youths are struggling with building close friendships and basic social skills (Twenge, 2017). Our children demonstrate deep caring about the world and each other, but research also suggests that they are significantly more vulnerable to mental health struggles (Twenge, 2019). The need to teach our children empathy and compassion skills, while also educating them about emotional flexibility and sup-porting the development of the full scope of social-emotional skills, has never been more evident.

The Caring Child: Raising Empathetic and Emotionally Intelligent Children was written to provide a resource for parents and educators that explains the underpinnings of empathy and compassion, and offers clear and concise recommendations for supporting the healthy development of these skills in our children. Covering topics that include empathy formation in the brain, how social-emotional skills enhance the overall functioning of children, and ways to support the development of healthy empathy and compassion skills from birth through adulthood, *The Caring Child* is a must-read book for today's parents.

How to Use This Book

The Caring Child is specifically designed to be an easy-to-use resource for parents and educators. Part I: Caring in a Digital World begins our journey through empathy and emotional flexibility by analyzing the current generation of children, iGen. The section con-tinues with an evaluation of the definitions of empathy and compassion. Part II: Caring and Emotional Intelligence increases our understanding of empathy and compassion through a deeper look at positive psychological skills, including resilience, emotional flexibility, and strengths practices. Part III: Empathy in Action brings everything together with scenarios and role-plays that address the home, school, and community environments.

Each chapter includes specific focus topics that highlight some of the most pressing issues of today, including the impact of social media on our children, how empathy develops within neurodiverse populations, and the argument against empathy. Tips for parents, role-plays pulled from years of coaching parents and children, and evidence-based strategies provide readers with the tools needed to positively impact children. Chapters end with "Cultivating Caring Action Steps" designed to help parents take specific steps to address compassion and empathy development in their children.

More than a book to quietly sit and read through once, *The Caring Child* is a companion to use on your parenting journey. As different situations arise, reference the appropriate section of the book to access specific tips and ideas to help you address your child's unique needs.

A Word to Educators

Although *The Caring Child* is explicitly written for parents, I wrote it with the needs of teachers, school counselors, mental health professionals, and school administrators in mind. Each chapter includes a "Whiteboard Workshop" section that addresses empathy and compassion within the school environment. Covering topics that range from the impact of technology on social development, creating caring classrooms, and teaching compassion at school, *The Caring Child* presents specific information, strategies, and tips to encourage empathy and compassion development within the context of learning and education.

Chapter 7: Empathy at School also addresses empathy at school through the use of school-based scenarios and role-plays developed through focus groups with educators across the United States. I hope that *The Caring Child* will positively impact students, providing a much-needed resource to both educators and parents.

A Word to Children and Teens

I know what you're thinking—here is another parenting book my parents are going to use "on" me. That is not what *The Caring Child* is all about. This book is for your parents to use "with" you, a tool to encourage deeper and more meaningful relationships within the entire family. If the topic interests you, read it along with your parents. Use the information together. Discover ways to increase empathy and compassion in your family. And then use the same information out in the world. We need you.

PART I

Caring in a Digital World

WE live in interesting times: News spreads around the world instantly, as social media is used to inform and inflict horrific pain. Our children and teens seem less resilient somehow, less able to handle life's adversities. Parents and educators both express frustration about our youth taking less and less responsibility for themselves and their actions.

As a school psychologist, I have witnessed the change in our children firsthand—I've seen the increase in aggression and defiance in our classrooms, the struggles between adults and children, and the attempts for schools to delve more and more into enhancing social-emotional development among children and adults.

At first, it would be easy to discount the changes as typical differences between generations, an expected generational gap. But there is nothing typical about this gap.

In this section, you will learn about the current generation of children, iGen. You will see why the differences in this generation pose unique challenges to how we parent and educate our children. You will also learn about the varying definitions of empathy and compassion, and how this impacts our understanding of caring.

DOI: 10.4324/9781003238751-2

Welcome to a New Generation

*Today's children confuse me somewhat. I think they show greater
capacity for empathy, and yet they are more detached from others
and more willing to bully each other online. I don't get it.*

—*Parent of a teen*

WALK down the hallway of today's high schools and you'll see
students engaging in conversations, laughing with friends, and hur-
rying to class. Elementary campuses look similar, with wide-eyed
students clumped in groups, laughing and interacting. Walk through
a crowded mall and things look a little different—children with
their eyes fixed on screens, parents talking on the phone or scrolling
through their texts as they rush from place to place. Conversations are
clipped, ranging from mild detachment to frustrated quips. Parents
say that life has gotten too busy and that children have forgotten the
simple pleasures of childhood. Children say that parents don't understand today's world. Children wrestle with their own technology use,
while also expressing frustration about how much their parents are
on their phones. Educators speak about cell phone usage in school

7

DOI: 10.4324/9781003238751-3

and the rise in behavioral challenges, all while struggling with their own cell phone use in between classes.

Technology isn't the only change in the world. A 24-hour news cycle highlights the most aggressive events on the planet, the constant barrage of "fake news" that makes legitimate information difficult to ascertain, and the dichotomy of both an apparent lack of empathy in the world and the hypervigilance and emotional enmeshment of some parents. These factors have created uncertainty about how to best help our children.

Children have not changed substantively—as humans, we still develop in ways similar to the earliest theories of Jean Piaget and Erik Erikson. Childhood, however, has changed. The growth of technology, changes in culture and family structures, increases in adverse childhood experiences, and their impact on the lives of children have all created a world much different from the one most of us experienced as children. If predictions are correct, the changes are only beginning. Now, more than ever, we need to understand the current generation of children, the role of technology and its impact on social-emotional development, and how to nurture our children's resilience and emotional intelligence.

Defining iGen

Dr. Jean Twenge (2017), a leading generational researcher, defined the generation after Millennials as iGen. Loosely defined as those children born between 1995 and 2012, iGen (or Generation Z) is the first generation to not know a world without the smartphone. This has big implications, according to Twenge and others. In the research conducted by Twenge (2017) for her book *iGen: Why Today's Super-Connected Kids Are Growing Up Less Rebellious, More Tolerant, Less Happy—and Completely Unprepared for Adulthood*, she stated that the differences between iGen and previous generations are significant and point to major shifts in how humans interact with the world.

Welcome to a New Generation

Let's start with a simple question: At what age did you get your driver's license? How about your first job? What about dating—when did you go out on your first date? Chances are that each of these events occurred during your high school years. This is not so for iGen. According to Twenge (2017), children today are growing up slower, experiencing many of the "firsts" well in to their 20s. The long-term impact of this is only beginning to be recognized. Children are entering college less prepared on a social level. With the lack of experience comes increased concern by parents about safety and decision making. Students are more vulnerable, with less practice making difficult decisions involving dating, sex, drug and alcohol use, and more. Although some of this may feel like a relief, the lack of experience can set up difficult situations for children in early adulthood.

Growing up more slowly isn't the only difference between iGen and previous generations. Twenge (2017) identified 10 key areas in which this generation varies from previous generations. The biggest shift comes from the increase in technology usage. iGen is super-connected to the digital world. Internet and smartphone use is up, and TV viewing is down. Ninety-five percent of adolescents in America report having Internet and smartphone access. More importantly, 45% of those children report being on their devices "constantly" (Anderson & Jiang, 2018). This percentage is staggering. Eighty percent of today's teens are on social media sites regularly (Stafford, 2018), including Facebook, Instagram, and Snapchat.

All of this social media connection is not beneficial, according to Twenge (2019; Twenge & Campbell, 2018). Decreases in happiness, increases in anxiety and depression, and increases in suicidal ideations have been associated with the increases in tech use, especially smartphones. Our tech-savvy children are struggling, and although smartphones have not been shown to cause the difficulties, there does appear to be a connection.

Additional differences between iGen and other generations include changes in opinions about marriage and childbirth, with both occurring at later ages; differences in social-emotional wellness largely related to perceived lack of social connections; and underdeveloped social skills. Increased safety related to decreases in risky behaviors like drug and alcohol use, and increases in social tolerance and diversity, are also trends within the iGen generation. All in all, iGen is substantively different from the preceding generations.

Beyond iGen

The generational differences between iGen and other generations don't appear to end with this group. Early marketing research into the generation of children born after 2012, currently referred to as Generation Alpha, suggests that the impact of technology on our children is only beginning. An early survey of parents of young children, conducted by Hotwire (2018), indicated that young children know their way around technology. According to the survey of more than 8,000 parents, children value tech above most other things, including toys and pets. Further, more than 65% of the parents surveyed said that their children's opinions influenced tech buying decisions.

As technology use increases with future generations, it is reasonable to assume the current concerns around technology addiction, reduced prosocial behaviors, and increased health concerns will remain or grow. Parents and educators need to support our youth as we all try to wrap our minds around what our digital age means for the social-emotional well-being of all of us.

Implications for Emotional Intelligence Development

Clearly the impact of technology isn't going away. As more and more children are born into this digital world, parents will continue to seek resources to help negate some of the negative impacts of our digital world—most of which we are only just beginning to understand. Early research suggests that the technology use has resulted in less happiness and more emotional distress among our children (Twenge, Joiner, Rogers, & Martin, 2018). One reason for this could be the decreased opportunities for real-time social interactions. As children spend less and less time together, the development of interpersonal processes is delayed. This impacts perspective-taking, emotional development, and compassion and empathy development, among other things. The delays in these skills then result in a weakening of resiliency, which decreases coping mechanisms for stress and anxiety. It is easy to see why today's youth are less happy. Changing this trajectory will require a shift in how we nurture the development of emotional intelligence competencies.

In addition to fostering more happiness, developing social-emotional skills will also prepare our children for the future. Employers have indicated the need for workplace skills amenable to the changing face of business. Competencies like critical thinking and problem solving, creativity, social intelligence, cognitive flexibility, compassion, and emotional intelligence have been highlighted more than the standard profession-specific skills as necessary in tomorrow's work force.

The Caring Child focuses on the development of the skills needed to build resilience, nurture empathy and compassion, and develop emotional intelligence, or EQ. This is what our children need now. This is what the world needs.

Screen Time and Psychological Well-Being

Twenge (2017) warned of an impending mental health crisis among our youth due, in part, to smartphones and the influence of technology. Despite Twenge's concerns, researchers are divided as to the impact of technology on mental health and psychological well-being (Stiglic & Viner, 2019; Straker, Zabatiero, Danby, Thorpe, & Edwards, 2019). Some articles emphatically link screen time to negative mental health outcomes (Babic et al., 2017; Twenge et al., 2018), while others are less certain (Odgers, 2018; Przybylski & Weinstein, 2019). In an effort to deepen the research into the impact of screen time on psychological well-being, Twenge and Campbell (2018) conducted a large-scale population survey to help examine the associations between screen time (including cell phones, electronic devices, computers, gaming, and TV) and psychological well-being (including positive relationships, emotional stability, emotional regulation, and diagnosed mental health conditions like anxiety, depression, and mood disorders). Results of the study were significant and, in my mind, laid to rest the debate. Increased screen time and decreases in psychological well-being go hand in hand. The more children use tablets, cell phones, gaming apps, and social media, the more they struggle with emotional regulation, social skill development, anxious-like behaviors, and even depression. Recent additional research confirms this, especially with regard to adolescents and gaming (Zink, Belcher, Kechter, Stone, & Leventhal, 2019). Additional concerns can be found with physical health when you consider the increases in a sedentary lifestyle that often accompany increased screen time.

This information throws parents into a difficult position. We live in a digital world, and barring some futuristic, dystopian event, that isn't going to change. Teaching our children balance around technology, particularly screen time, isn't just good parenting; it's vital to our children's mental health.

But what does balance mean? Should we ban all screens, controlling everything we can about technology use and our children. Some parents may answer "Yes!" Personally, I find that to be not only unrealistic, but also impractical and unnecessary. Screen time isn't something to fear. Yes, there are significant negative effects of screen time, social media, and smartphone usage However, there is no way to completely remove these from your child's world—at least not permanently. I recommend a balanced, commonsense approach.

The American Academy of Pediatrics (AAP, 2016) has specific guidelines regarding screen time for young children under 5:
- Birth to 18 months: None, with the exception of video chat applications.

- 18–24 months: Less than one hour/day of educational programming that is developmentally appropriate.
- 2–5 years: Up to one hour/day of educational programming that is developmentally appropriate and viewed with parents.
- 6 years and up: "Consistent limits."

Although the guidelines through age 5 are specific and appropriate based on the research, the guidelines for use above age 5 leave parents wondering exactly what "consistent" limits should mean.

I recommend that parents begin by establishing when screen time is not allowed. Mealtimes, while driving, after bedtime, and when focused attention is needed are all examples of when screen time is not beneficial and can actually be harmful. Once some boundaries and limits are determined, expectations regarding what screen time can be used for are essential. Specific discussion around social media and gaming is important, especially as children become adolescents and are afforded more freedoms. Finally, specific conversations about digital citizenship, including online bullying and cyber threats, need to be consistently held. Taking predetermined digital breaks, or times when everyone agrees to go "off the grid," can help maintain healthy balance and avoid tech addictions.

Screen time does not have to be the enemy. Technology isn't all bad. It is the unbalanced approach we have taken with screen time and the rapid rise of technology that has led to some of the concerns today. Take back control and put limits for use in place that all household members can agree to (that includes the adults), and screen time can cease to become the hot-button issue it is in most households.

For a great family plan you can create, check out the Family Media Plan available at https://www.healthychildren.org/English/media/pages/default.aspx.

Whiteboard Workshop: iGen at School

This chapter has focused on the latest generation of children to come through the school system, iGen. The eldest members of this group, born around 1995, are graduating from college. The next generation, Generation Alpha, is suspected to have similar qualities as iGen. As discussed earlier, there are significant ramifications related to technology with iGen and later generations. The impact of this digital age is not only felt at home, but also within schools.

Ask any group of teachers about this generation of students and they will tell you that this group is different. Based on my focus groups, students today struggle with task initiation and completion and require significant levels of support for nearly everything. Students display more mental health concerns, especially in the areas of stress and anxiety. These findings aren't surprising; they are consistent with Twenge's (2017) research.

iGen is considered the safest generation we've experienced. Yet these students are less mentally safe. Psychologists have expressed concern regarding soaring suicide rates (more than three-fold for girls over the last decade) and depression (Stafford, 2018). Students aren't social outside of school much, are sleep deprived, and are overly attached to their smartphones. All of this points to significant problems with social-emotional wellness that have permeated schools and homes alike.

What can schools do to help stem the impending mental health crisis? It starts will a full understanding of the needs of this generation, coupled with action to work in partnership with parents to support children. Embed social-emotional learning into the classroom and school. Teach strategies to improve attention and motivation. Show the connection between learning, mental health, and future outcomes. All of this will start to support the needs of this new generation. Tip Sheet 1: Supporting Students in a Digital Age provides additional tips for schools as they grapple with this new generation and those to come.

TIP SHEET 1
Supporting Students in a Digital Age
●━━━━━━━━━━━━━━━━━━━━━━━━━━━━━━━━━━━━━●

iGen is here. These students rarely read books or e-mails, but they devour social media. They are stressed out and isolated, but passionate about the world and driven to make it better. They are diverse in every way possible. And they have challenged the status quo of how we teach.

Here are a few ways we can be responsive to the educational needs of this generation:

» Have flexibility in the content.

» Include projects and activities that are student driven and meaningful.

» Embed social-emotional learning skills into content areas.

» Individualize education as much as possible.

» Take a balanced approach to technology. Use the following considerations as guidance:

  › Appropriate for the content (vs. inappropriate): Make sure the activity requires technology use to enhance learning, not just make things easier. Consider developmental appropriateness as well.

  › Adds value and meaning to learning (vs. passive participation in an activity): Consider the difference between using tablets and smartphones to record movies, take pictures, and enhance an activity versus the passive use of a gaming app to do drill-and-kill math calculations.

  › Empowers student engagement in the activity (vs. enabling the student): Consider the use of technology as a substitute for language. Is the technology empowering communication, or is it blocking the development of language in general?

iGen is here. Technology is here. Neither are bad. But living in a digital world does have potential negative consequences we are only beginning to understand. We must acknowledge the struggles if we are going to give our children what they need to best function in our future world.

The rest of the book focuses on building social-emotional skills as a way to address the needs of a digital world. With chapters that focus on the biology of caring, developing resilience, and building emotional intelligence, it is my hope that you will receive the information and resources you need to nurture your children, increase happiness, and decrease the negative wellness outcomes currently observed in the world.

Cultivating Caring Action Steps

In this chapter, you learned about iGen and future generations. For these generations, the impact of technology cannot be emphasized enough. Smartphones and social media have shaped how children in the developed nations interact with the world. Your action steps for this chapter similarly focus on the impact of technology in your home. Over the next week or so, take a few moments to focus on how technology is used within your home. Technology includes all screen time (TV, computers, tablets, and smartphones), as well as the use of social media and gaming apps. The following are three action steps to take that will help you recognize what your current technology usage is and how to ensure screen time and technology balance:

1. Take inventory of the screens, devices, and technology in your home, indicating the type of technology, who the primary users of the technology are, and the average amount of usage daily or weekly.
2. Develop technology goals regarding usage and a plan to reduce use as necessary based on the information you gained in Action #1. Develop technology use rules with your family

that address usage and times when technology is not to be used (i.e., during meals and after bedtime).

3. Schedule monthly digital breaks when all members of the household go "off the grid." This can be one day a month, one weekend a month, or more. Use this time to reconnect as a family and build empathy and compassion skills through in-person communication.

After evaluating technology, take some time to focus on relationships. Begin by taking a look at the relationships within your household, both those with the children and those with other adults. Deepening the positive relationships within the home environment will provide the needed foundation to grow social-emotional skills, including empathy and compassion. The following are action steps to take that will help you define the current state of relationships in the home and take the necessary actions to deepen them:

1. List the relationships in the household, including adult-child, child-child, and adult-adult. Define the relationships and their positive aspects. If there are concerns within any of the relationships, list those concerns as well. This is not a place to feel any guilt or shame regarding the state of any relationship. For example, if you have a teenager in the house, you may list some difficulties being able to simply talk with him or her. This is developmentally normal. It is also something that would benefit from some focused attention to deepen the relationship and improve any communication struggles.

2. List two or three things you can do to improve any of the relationship difficulties you listed. Also list things you can do to continue strong relationships already present within the household.

3. Using the list you created in Action #2, schedule specific actions to ensure their completion. Using the difficult relationship with a teenager as an example, you may have listed a mother-daughter date as something you want to do to help improve the relationship with the teen. It is important to

actually schedule the time, make plans, etc. Otherwise, life has a tendency of rolling on, and we may never take the time to have the date and focus on the relationship with our adolescent child. As you take the actions you've scheduled, focus on understanding the other person, trying to see the world from his or her perspective, and deepening your relationships. This will help with the work ahead.

2

Empathy and Compassion Defined

The meaning of empathy has really changed over the years for me.
I used to think of it as something you either have or don't. Now,
I'm not so sure. I wonder how much of it can be taught or based
on your environment.

—Elementary school teacher

EMPATHY, compassion, self-compassion, kindness, caring—
these five words are some of the most highly used today as buzz-
words that represent ideals. When I ask parents and educators what
skill they think is most important today, most respond with one of
the words above. When I probe further, I usually get answers that
involve all five words overlapping and combining to form a singular
concept. The point parents and educators are making is clear: There is
a need for more caring and kindness in today's world. There is a second point being made as well—there is little consensus as to what is
meant by the five words above, especially when it comes to empathy
and compassion. Yes, people indicate that they want more of these
attributes. But no one is really sure what that means.

19

DOI: 10.4324/9781003238751-4

Starting a conversation and nurturing "caring" in others start, therefore, with defining the skills most commonly associated with caring: empathy and compassion. I thought this would be an easy task.

I was wrong.

Defining Empathy

Empathy definitions vary highly, even within research circles. This makes understanding the available research regarding empathy difficult, as you must first understand the theoretical model of empathy used in the research. de Waal (2009), one of the pioneers in defining empathy, traced the origins of empathy, including the ideas of emotional mimicry and emotional contagions, back more than 100 million years. Further research points to empathy as an evolutionary prosocial value within primates and nonprimates, with studies that indicate the presence of mirrored emotional responses across species, contexts, and distances.

In 1873, philosopher Robert Vischer defined empathy as "feeling into," or the act of projecting oneself into another and feeling that person's emotions (Stevens & Woodruff, 2018). During a recent focus group, one of my participants defined empathy as a "great act of emotional imagination"—the act of imagining another's emotions based on environmental and social cues. This idea of "feeling into" certainly aligns with the most common notion of empathy as being the ability to experience another's feelings.

With modern research into the construct of empathy, new definitions and models have arisen. Singer and Lamm (2009) viewed empathy as a complex construct involving four distinct processes: emotional sharing, emotional mimicry, a mental representation of another's emotions (theory of mind), and differentiation between self and others. Other models include a distinction between emotional empathy and cognitive empathy (Decety & Jackson, 2004) and a three-process model of empathy involving emotional sharing, empathetic concern, and perspective-taking (Decety, Norman, Berntson, & Cacioppo, 2012). Regulation of emotional response has also been included in some models of empathy, folding into the empathetic concern constructs (Baron-Cohen, 2011) Regardless of how you attempt to define empathy, research is clear that it is a multifaceted idea.

I take a more eclectic approach to defining empathy. Building on all of the models above, I see empathy as a complex skill that involves both emotional and cognitive processes (affective and cognitive empathy). Within these processes are emotional awareness and sharing, empathetic responding on the emotional side, and theory of mind and perspective-taking on the cognitive side. Full maturation of this skill occurs developmentally over time and is dependent on the maturation of other social-emotional skills.

Defining Compassion

Empathy isn't the only aspect of caring that is difficult to define. Researchers have also struggled with compassion, a natural companion to empathy. Compassion is a newer idea in evolutionary study. Most researchers agree that the concept of caring for another and acting on that caring arose as a necessary component of community and species survival (Wang, 2005). Early religious texts highlighted the moral idea of being sensitive to the pain of others and doing something to help. Others have defined it as "feeling with" (as opposed to the empathy idea of "feeling into"; Goetz, Keltner, & Simon-Thomas, 2010).

Compassion is distinguished from empathy in most research and generally is more favorably viewed. The most common model involves three processes, including the brief experience of affective (or emotional) empathy, cognitive labeling of the others' emotions, and acting to alleviate the suffering of the other (Stevens & Woodruff, 2018). Essential in this construct is the idea of taking action. In my focus groups, this idea of action as being a defining feature of compassion was also expressed.

A more recent model posed by Singer and Klimecki (2014) views compassion as a subtype of empathy. In particular, these researchers defined compassion as a type of empathetic response within the processes involved in the larger construct of empathy (Decety et al., 2012). This is more in line with my perspective: compassion as part of the continuum of empathy that represents a matured aspect of an empathetic response.

It is important to note that there is biological evidence to suggest that compassion is a unique skill, involving different regions of the brain. It is a point made repeatedly by Paul Bloom (2016) in his case against empathy (see p. 23), as well as a point emphasized by other researchers. I will delve more into my model of empathy and emotional intelligence later in the book. For now, I will simply say that I view compassion as part of an empathetic response and, therefore, part of empathy.

Defining Self-Compassion

The last definition I would like to explore is self-compassion. This one is far easier. There is little debate in research circles regarding the construct of self-compassion. Defined within the extensive research of Neff (2003a, 2003b), compassion is comprised of three subcomponents: self-kindness (vs. self-judgement), mindfulness (vs. overidentification), and common humanity (vs. isolation). Self-compassion, then, involves the feeling of compassion turned inward, a mature empathetic response to oneself, present-moment awareness, and the feeling of shared connection to a larger community (or sense of belonging). I delve more deeply into self-compassion and its benefits in later chapters.

Empathy and Compassion Defined

The Argument Against Empathy

In 2016, Yale University researcher Paul Bloom presented his case against the construct of empathy in his critically-acclaimed book *Against Empathy: The Case for Rational Compassion*. Bloom explained that empathy, although a well-intentioned idea, does more harm than good. In fact, empathy may actually hinder your moral reasoning. It sounds strange after the current conversation about empathy, I know. But many of Bloom's ideas are supported by the research and deserve examination.

The crux of Bloom's (2016) ideas is in his definition of empathy as feeling the feeling of others fully. In this, he said, people experience high levels of distress, and there is nothing inherently beneficial in that. Bloom pointed out research that suggests that people experience more empathy if they can relate to the person they are trying to be empathetic with. Take the example of a car crash. Let's say you pass a horrible solo car crash and immediately feel bad for the driver involved—until you find out that the driver was drinking and that was why he crashed. Your feelings shift with that knowledge. Now you are angry. Your empathy for the situation dissipates because of the judgment you've placed on the driver's actions. This, according to Bloom, speaks to the biases inherent in empathy and why it is a bad model for morality.

Bloom (2016) continued by making a case for what he calls "rational compassion." By his definition, rational compassion involves the act of acknowledging another's feelings, but not necessarily becoming enmeshed in the feeling the way you do with empathy. After acknowledging the feelings, you take action to alleviate the other person's suffering and do so in a rational way. This, he argued, is a better model for virtue or morality. Bloom isn't saying empathy is bad. Rather he is saying it is flawed, limited. Compassion is better. Some researchers would agree.

For me, this is the wrong conversation. I don't think this is about a binary choice between empathy and compassion, emotions and reason, or feeling and responding. I think it is about emotional intelligence, the recognition of self and other, and the ability to positively contribute to the greater good of all, without sacrificing self.

A Model of Empathy

After reading the research and evaluating the varied ideas of empathy and compassion, I have a more unified view of how the mechanisms of empathy develop and work together. I agree that there are both cognitive processes and social-emotional processes at work. I also view empathy as something that develops or matures with experience and in line with the growth of an individual's emotional intelligence. Figure 1 shows what I think is an easy way to conceptualize how these factors work together.

Empathy, as you can see in the diagram, is the product of cognitive skills and social-emotional processes. When you are low on both, as is the case of individuals with particular mental health conditions or neurological impairments, you are likely to struggle to notice feelings at all—yours or anyone's. If your cognitive skills develop, but your social-emotional processes lag behind, you will likely be able to identify other's emotions from an intellectual place. In this stage, you may make judgments about what someone feels, correcting their feelings. You will not, most likely, actually feel someone else's feelings, however.

If, on the other hand, your social and emotional processes develop and your cognitive skills lag, you are likely to "feel into" another easily. However, your lack of cognitive skill development makes it difficult for you to differentiate your feelings from another's, resulting in enmeshment with others and a strong likelihood of becoming emotionally distressed due to another's feelings. Much of what Bloom (2016) talked about is this type of empathy—an immature, incomplete version of the skill.

The goal is full development and maturation of *both* cognitive and social-emotional skills and processes. When these are fully devel-

EQ

SEL Area: Social and emotional skills and processes →

	SEL Area: Social and emotional skills and processes →	

Top-left quadrant:

EQ Development: High cognitive skills; low social and emotional skill development

Empathetic Response: *"I know what feelings you should have, but I don't really 'feel' them, so I tend to judge your feelings and struggle to connect to your emotions."*

Potential Problems: high threat awareness; rigid responses; poor relationships; weak attachments

Needed Skills to Improve EQ: Focus on connections, relationship skills, and emotional awareness/regulation

Top-right quadrant:

EQ Development: High cognitive, social, and emotional skill development

Empathetic Response: *"I feel with you and hold no judgments about you or your feelings. I recognize the difference between self and other; I walk with you in your emotions from a place of compassion!"*

Potential Problems: None; this is fully developed EQ

Needed Skills to Improve EQ: Continue growth over the lifetime, building competencies to handle different problems

Bottom-left quadrant:

EQ Development: Limited cognitive, social, and emotional skill development

Empathetic Response: *"I don't feel feelings that much at all—yours, mine, anyone's."*

Potential Problems: Difficulty connecting socially; difficulty with connections or attachment

Needed Skills to Improve EQ: Concentrated focus on building all social-emotional, cognitive skills, starting with positive relationships/connections

Bottom-right quadrant:

EQ Development: Low cognitive skill development; high social and emotional skills development

Empathetic Response: *"I feel for you, becoming fully enmeshed in your emotions, often ending up in emotional distress because I struggle to differentiate you from me."*

Potential Problems: Enmeshment; emotional distress; overwhelm; anxiety

Needed Skills to Improve EQ: Focus on developing flexible thinking, awareness of self and other (theory of mind), inhibitory skills, and rational problem solving

← **SEL Area:** Cognitive skills and processes →

Figure 1. Empathy development model.

oped, you have the capacity to "feel with" another—experiencing the other's feelings and emotional context, while also differentiating self from other. You recognize that his or her feelings are his or hers, not yours. In doing so, you are able to walk with another through his or her emotional experience without judgment or distress. This is fully matured empathy. This, in my opinion, is what most people mean by compassion.

Interestingly, research into restorative practices of discipline, parenting styles, and the social environments of the brain follow a similar pattern to my model of empathy and EQ development (Saufler, 2011). Figure 2 shows the empathy model layered with restorative practices, parenting styles, and potential brain states. I believe this type of an integrated model clearly demonstrates how these factors—brain processes, environmental supports, and human interactions—influence the development of empathy, compassion, and, most importantly, emotional intelligence.

The purpose of this type of integrated model is to help both parents and educators understand how they can positively influence how children develop and provide them with the things needed to create a more caring world. Tip Sheet 2: Parenting For EQ provides some tips for helping children mature their cognitive skills and develop strong levels of empathy.

TIP SHEET 2
Parenting for EQ

There are several strategies you can use with children to develop social-emotional learning skills. Use the ideas below to help you as you nurture your child's skills:

» Developing Cognitive Skills:
  › Build puzzles, engage in language-based games, and do word searches together to help refine attention and cognitive flexibility skills.

Empathy and Compassion Defined

EQ

	SEL Area: Social and emotional skills and processes	**Social Environment:** Nurturing, relational, supportive
	Parenting/Teaching Style: AUTHORITARIAN **Discipline Approach:** Do TO; judgmental; punitive **EQ Development:** High cognitive skills; low social and emotional skill development **Empathetic Response:** *"I know what feelings you should have, but I don't really 'feel' them, so I tend to judge your feelings and struggle to connect to your emotions."* **Potential Problems:** high threat awareness; rigid responses; poor relationships; weak attachments **Needed Skills to Improve EQ:** Focus on connections, relationship skills, and emotional awareness/regulation	**Parenting/Teaching Style:** AUTHORITATIVE/RELATIONSHIP-FOCUSED **Discipline Approach:** Do WITH; relational; learning-focused **EQ Development:** High cognitive, social, and emotional skill development **Empathetic Response:** *"I feel with you and hold no judgments about you or your feelings. I recognize the difference between self and other; I walk with you in your emotions from a place of compassion!"* **Potential Problems:** None; this is fully developed EQ **Needed Skills to Improve EQ:** Continue growth over the lifetime, building competencies to handle different problems
	Parenting/Teaching Style: NEGLECTFUL/ABSENT **Discipline Approach:** Do nothing; ignore; nonresponsive **EQ Development:** Limited cognitive, social, and emotional skill development **Empathetic Response:** *"I don't feel feelings that much at all—yours, mine, anyone's."* **Potential Problems:** Difficulty connecting socially, difficulty with connections or attachment **Needed Skills to Improve EQ:** Concentrated focus on building all social-emotional, cognitive skills, starting with positive relationships/connections	**Parenting/Teaching Style:** PERMISSIVE/INDULGENT **Discipline Approach:** Do FOR; lenient; makes excuses **EQ Development:** Low cognitive skill development; high social and emotional skills development **Empathetic Response:** *"I feel for you, becoming fully enmeshed in your emotions, often ending up in emotional distress because I struggle to differentiate you from me."* **Potential Problems:** Enmeshment, emotional distress, overwhelm, anxiety. **Needed Skills to Improve EQ:** Focus on developing flexible thinking, awareness of self and other (theory of mind), inhibitory skills, rational problem solving
	Social Environment: Limits, rational, boundaries **SEL Area:** Cognitive skills and processes	

Figure 2. Integrated empathy development model. Adapted from Saufler, 2011.

TIP SHEET 2, *continued*

> › Engage in creativity exercises and creative play. Make this a purely social activity (no technology) for an even bigger impact.
>
> › Practice goal setting with your children.

» Developing Social and Relational Skills:

> › Teach social awareness through books and media. Talk about what makes the various characters do what they do and say what they say.
>
> › Practice conflict mediation skills together using role-plays.
>
> › Nurture perspective-taking through improv games.

» Developing Emotional Skills:

> › Develop emotional awareness through mindfulness activities.
>
> › Build emotional regulation skills through relaxation and other coping techniques.
>
> › Use books and media, including your children's fandoms, to delve deeper into emotional awareness and regulation.

» Developing Character Skills:

> › Read books about character strengths and talk about how the different strengths were demonstrated.
>
> › Use superheroes to talk about character strengths. Have your children identify the strengths most commonly used by the characters.
>
> › Engage in regular strengths-based practices with your children.

TIP SHEET 2, *continued*

» Developing Mindsets:

› Teach your children about perseverance and a growth mindset.

› Use biographies of people your children are interested in to teach real-life stories of grit and determination.

› Identify examples of optimism and a growth mindset in movies and other media.

The Case for Caring

Between the difficulties in defining empathy and compassion and the compelling arguments of Bloom (2016), you may wonder if focusing on empathy and compassion is worthwhile. I would say "yes." As I mentioned previously, I think Bloom asks the wrong questions. This isn't a black-and-white choice. This is much more complicated, as the empathy model indicates. It is about developing all social-emotional skills—cognitive skills, emotional and social processes, character strengths and mindset—all with the goal of enhancing caring in individuals and groups. By focusing on developing social-emotional competencies, you develop emotional intelligence. This, in turn, enhances resiliency and all of the skills required for caring.

No matter which model of empathy you use, whether you see compassion as part of empathy or something different, and whether one is more important than the other, by focusing on the development of all of these skills in your children, you are giving them the assets that they need to combat the negative aspects of living in a digital world. You are supporting their desire to make the world a better place, something we know is important to iGen (Twenge, 2017).

Our children already care about the world. Now they need the skills to be able to express that caring in productive ways. Supporting both empathy and compassion, as well as the other aspects of emotional intelligence, gives them everything they need to shape the world into something more tolerant and kinder.

Whiteboard Workshop: The Academic Benefits of Caring

To understand how and why learning occurs within a classroom, one must first understand basic brain functioning. The human brain serves one primary purpose: survival. It does this by safeguarding energy when it perceives threat or danger. Think of an emotionally charged event. It is difficult to rationally think in such a state; your fight-or-flight stress response kicks in, and your primary focus is surviving the threat, nothing more. Your brain is not as available to new learning. Your focus is not on novel problem solving. Instead, your brain relies on previously learned patterns of response in order to meet the demands of the moment without overusing available energy.

Now, think about a classroom. Every moment of every day, students make decisions about whether the new information being received (the content they are being taught) should get filtered to the prefrontal cortex, or "thinking brain," or to the more reactive parts of the brain where fight-or-flight responses live, etc. This decision is mediated by a person's emotions in the moment. If you are calm and relaxed, the information is filtered to the thinking brain. If your stress responses are activated, the information goes straight to the threat centers, the reactive parts of the brain (Willis, 2018). For students, stress can be triggered by everything from boredom, to lack of relevance in the material, to interpersonal difficulties with the teacher or other students, to poor resilience related to underdeveloped social-emotional skills.

How can you ensure that students are as calm as possible, in order to learn new information? Focus on creating caring environments that promote compassion. Developing healthy relationships with students, balancing academic challenges with achievable goals, promoting prosocial behaviors, and communicating empathy and compassion to students have all been shown to increase student engagement and create the environment needed for learning (Willis, 2018).

How significant is the impact in creating caring environments that enhance social-emotional development in children? Research correlates positive school climates with improved academic achievement. The impact is even more significant when social-emotional learning programs are embedded within the positive school climate. In one meta-analysis, academic gains of 13 percentage points were found when a caring environment and explicit social-emotional learning were woven into the academic setting (Durlak, Weissberg, Dymnicki, Taylor, & Schellinger, 2011).

Managing the environment to foster resilience, academic risk-taking and social-emotional growth is about establishing sustainable structures that promote learning. This is the foundation of a caring classroom.

Rooted in the research around trauma and trauma-sensitive classrooms, a caring classroom includes the following components:
- positive relationships between adults and children,
- clear expectations for behavior,
- predictable and consistent responses from adults, and
- a sense of agency for students.

Let's examine each more closely.

Building positive relationships between adults and students is a key aspect of the caring classroom. Through these relationships, trust and safety are established, which lower the brain's threat response. Connections enable students to gain a sense of belonging, which can strengthen self-compassion. Positive relationships also allow for empathy modeling and strengthening of EQ skills.

Clear expectations of behavior enable students to know ahead of time what is expected of them. This also works to lower inhibitions to learning and prime the brain to accept new information. Reviewing the expectations repeatedly helps students learn and practice response flexibility as they navigate the social milieu of the classroom.

Predictable and consistent responses from adults help create a sense of safety for students. This enhances learning through reducing threat responses. Also, predictable responses often remove the emotional overload and turn behavioral missteps into viable opportunities for growth and learning.

A sense of agency for students refers to opportunities to express student voice and contribute to the classroom community. Agency primes learning by making information relevant and meaningful to the student, leading to more student autonomy with learning. It also contributes to the classroom community as a whole, setting the stage to refine empathy and compassion skill development.

The caring classroom is essential for learning, especially with the needs of our iGen students. Cultivating a caring classroom isn't difficult. I would guess that many of these components are already in place. Tip Sheet 3: Strategies That Cultivate a Caring Environment includes more ideas to make classrooms conducive to learning.

TIP SHEET 3
Strategies That Cultivate a Caring Environment

» Focus on cultivating positive relationships first and foremost.
» Collaboratively establish norms and expectations for behavior.
» Establish trust and safety through predictable reactions and open communication.
» Address conflict in a calm, empathy-focused manner.
» Assume positive intent.
» Balance the needs of all people.

The definition of *caring* has changed over time. Empathy and compassion are viewed as distinct processes and aspects of a continuum. This confusion has led both terms to become catch-all phrases that point to the ability to understand, feel, and react to another's feelings and experiences. Although landing on one definition is important, the more important issue is how to nurture and develop empathy and compassion, and how this helps our children.

Over the next chapters, I will explore the biology of empathy and compassion and present ways to support the development of these skills in our children, all with the goal of improved wellness.

Cultivating Caring Action Steps

Chapter 2 focused defining both empathy and compassion. You examined how these terms came to influence positive psychology and whether or not empathy could actually be a bad thing. For your action steps, we turn our focus to increasing kindness at home. By laying a foundation of kindness through our interactions with each other, we can nurture our emotional intelligence. The following three action steps help establish empathy and compassion within the home environments:

1. Have a conversation with your children and the other adults about the meaning of empathy and compassion. This can be accomplished through a family meeting or similar method. Discuss what it means to be kind and have a caring home.

2. Together, establish family expectations with regards to empathy and compassion. Define what it means to be kind at home and how each member of the house is expected to behave. Make sure that children provide input on this—they often can define this better than we can as they often do a similar activity within their classrooms. Once you've established expectations, consider making a sign or poster to help everyone remember the agreements made.

3. Discuss as a family how to correct empathy and compassion errors at home. Empower children and adults alike to help everyone remember to follow the expectations listed in Action #2. Role-play and practice both how to correct behavior and how to respond when being corrected. This will help script expectations and prepare for inevitable corrections that will be needed in the future.

After setting expectations, it is time to examine boundaries. It may be hard to maintain healthy boundaries in today's culture. Taking the three action steps below can help you and your family develop appropriate limits.

1. Take stock of the current state of your boundaries. This is the time for clear, honest reflection. Have you established clear rules and consequences within the household structure? Do you stick to those limits and impose the consequences as needed? Are you emotionally enmeshed with your children—do you get overly distraught when they are distraught? Does the line between your emotions and your children's emotions get blurred? Do you focus on your thoughts, feelings, and emotions when dealing with a difficult situation with your children, or are you focused on your child's thoughts, feelings, and emotions?

2. Once you've taken stock of the current reality of boundaries in your household, make a list of the things you would like to improve. Pick one or two of the listed items that are most important to you and make a plan to take action.

3. Use Tip Sheet 4: Establishing Healthy Boundaries to ensure that you have developed expectations and consequences and are following through consistently.

TIP SHEET 4
Establishing Healthy Boundaries

» Establish clear expectations for behavior.

» Mean what you say, and say what you mean.

» Follow through on all consequences — every time.

» Be clear on your emotions versus your child's emotions.

» Let your children fail.

» Support your children, but don't rescue your children.

» Natural consequences are a good thing.

PART II

Caring and Emotional Intelligence

IN this section, you will move from defining empathy and compassion to the larger conversation of emotional intelligence and emotional flexibility. Pulling on positive psychological research, this section focuses on developing all areas of social-emotional learning skills, especially those areas that are needed for compassion and empathy.

In addition to the focus on developing emotional intelligence overall, special focus is given to both response flexibility (the ability to intentionally choose your response to a given situation) and what I call emotional flexibility (the ability to feel and respond in contextually appropriate ways to a variety of situations). It is my belief that one of the reasons the iGen generation struggles so deeply with resilience and anxious-like behaviors is due to a lack of flexibility in responding to environmental stimuli. This section explores that concern and provides resources to help teach children how to respond to difficult situations in healthy ways.

The section finishes with specific strategies in the areas of mindfulness, strengths-based practices, and compassion training as a foundation for supporting the development of mental wellness and strong emotional intelligence in our youth.

 DOI: 10.4324/9781003238751-5

3

Empathy and
Resilience

I think there is a lack of resilience in the world. We just don't seem as able to overcome difficult events anymore. I don't know if that relates to changes in empathy, but it sure seems to result in less empathy.
—Elementary school teacher and father of two young children

ONE of my first memories of empathy happened on my first ocean dive when I was 11. At that time, my mom was my entire world. Where she went, I wanted to go. What she did, I wanted to do. She was my everything. As a family, we decided to become certified in scuba diving. My mom, dad, and I took the classes and practiced using the equipment in a pool.

On the day of our first ocean dive, I'd never been more excited. This is something I'd looked forward to for years. I was already fully geared up and in the water when my mom jumped off the boat. As her body hit the cold water, she experienced a full-blown panic attack. I watched in horror as her face blanched and she struggled to breathe. In that moment, I felt everything she felt. As her heart

DOI: 10.4324/9781003238751-6

pounded, so did mine. As she gasped for breath, my lungs clenched. It was terrifying.

Mom's panic attack didn't last long. The dive masters and my dad got her back onto the boat and helped her to relax as I treaded water and watched. Within moments, it seemed, my dad was back in the water, and I was expected to continue the dive. Not wanting to disappoint anyone, I complied. I pushed aside the feelings and followed my dad into the quiet world of the ocean. My thoughts were not on the beautiful views in front of me, however. They were on my mom and the fear I saw lodged in her eyes. It is something I've never forgotten. In our shared experience, her panic was mine. We were emotionally enmeshed in that experience. And this is the "problem" with empathy—sometimes when the skill is not fully matured, our empathy for another leads to our distress. I wasn't able to complete the required tests on that dive. And I never received my dive certification.

You may wonder why I chose to use this story to start a conversation about resilience. After all, I just pointed out a very real example of the downside of empathy. It is precisely for that reason that I use it. Empathy, as I've mentioned earlier, is a part of a broader collection of competencies that make up emotional intelligence. As you develop your social-emotional skills, including empathy and compassion, you gain a natural buffer against some of the unforeseen complications and emotional distress brought on by empathy. You mature your empathetic response and strengthen your resilience.

In this chapter, you will examine the components of resilience and emotional intelligence and how these skills mature your empathetic response. This information will help you support your children as they develop much-needed resilience. You will give them a buffer against the mental health challenges facing iGen.

Defining Resilience

Resilience is commonly defined as the ability to bounce back after a setback. It is the full integration of your brain's various processes working in harmony to regulate your fear and threat responses, manage your emotions, engage your prefrontal cortex to problem solve, tune into your empathy and compassion to reach out socially, and exercise flexibility in how you respond to the specific event occurring in ways that will result in the best outcomes. In short, resilience is the activation of your emotional intelligence to promote healthy adaptation to your environment that increases your chances for survival.

Resiliency taps into all of your social-emotional competencies, including cognitive responses (attention, inhibition, executive functioning, and problem solving), emotional processes (awareness, regulation, empathy, and perspective-taking), interpersonal processes (relationship skills, social awareness, conflict management), mindset (grit, perseverance, growth mindset), and character strengths (Jones et al., 2017). By nurturing these skills, you can improve your resilience and the resilience of your children to better handle life's challenges. Tip Sheet 5: Growing Social-Emotional Learning shows ways to develop social-emotional competencies in your children, with ideas for preschoolers and adolescents alike.

TIP SHEET 5
Growing Social-Emotional Learning (SEL)

» Focus on teaching emotional awareness and regulation. Start with teaching an emotional vocabulary.

» Teach social cues and prosocial behaviors to children. Play "emotional detective" games to deepen skills.

» Practice perspective-taking skills. Use literature and other media to explore other points of view.

» Focus on building coping strategies to help with regulation of stress and anxiety.

» Teach creative problem-solving skills and conflict resolution skills.

TIP SHEET 5, *continued*

» Develop and practice oral communication skills.

Note. Adapted from Fonseca, 2015.

Improving Resilience

When the brain is working at peak performance, your resiliency skills match the levels of adversity you face. Your brain's integration and communication are intact, and you are able to cope and adapt to whatever comes your way. Sometimes, however, things are not working at their best. Past traumas, the severity of your environmental stressors, and the underdevelopment of your emotional intelligence skills can adversely impact your resilience. This is what the research says is occurring with our youth—deficits in social-emotional development brought about by unhealthy uses of technology have stalled emotional and interpersonal processes, changing some of the resilience responses demonstrated by our children (Twenge, 2017). Unfortunately, the unhealthy patterns of responding to adverse experiences can get hardwired into their brains, and their overall resilience diminishes. This may explain the rising rates of anxiety and depression among adolescents currently.

The good news is that this is changeable. Our children can learn different response patterns. They can develop grit and perseverance, sharpen their empathy and compassion skills, and change their resilience.

Linda Graham (2013), author of the award-winning book on resilience, *Bouncing Back: Rewiring Your Brain for Maximum Resilience and Well-Being*, defined multiple processes within a resilient response. According to Graham (2013, 2018), resilience involves a somatic component, an emotional component, a relational component that involves empathy and compassion, and a reflective component. Developing these areas is key to improving resiliency.

Empathy and Resilience

The somatic aspect of resilience involves a mind-body connection that can be activated to manage the biological responses to threat generated through our fight-or-flight response. Graham (2013) recommended using movement, breath, and touch to quell the activation of our amygdala and manage our fight-or-flight responses. Kelly McGonigal (2015), author of *The Upside of Stress: Why Stress Is Good for You, and How to Get Good at It*, similarly recommended changing our definitions of stress from maladaptive to adaptive as a way of managing our somatic response to stressful events. Using relaxation strategies focused on calming the physical signs of distress can help change our response to adversity and nurture resilience.

In addition to mind-body responses to adversity, Graham (2013, 2018) recommended refining emotional and interpersonal processes as a way to rewire your resilience. Developing emotional awareness through mindfulness and similar practices will not only allow you to recognize how you are responding to a given situation, but also enable you to see times when your brain may be incorrectly labeling information.

Yes, that is correct—your brain can and does lie to you at times. It is hardwired toward threat perception, meaning that the brain disproportionally attends to things it finds threatening. Not only that, but the brain often misinterprets information in order to maintain status quo. In my book, *Letting Go* (Fonseca, 2017), I referred to this as the brain's cons. These cons lead to cognition errors and are a primary force behind anxiety and similar concerns. Recognizing and correcting misperceptions and cognition errors is essential to nurturing resilience and maturing our social-emotional skills.

Chapter 5 focuses on a variety of strategies that nurture emotional and interpersonal processes, including mindfulness and strengths awareness. These practices will enable you and your children to change your responses to adversity and improve resilience.

Empathy and Resilience

In addition to nurturing mind-body responses to adversity and developing emotional processes, empathy and compassion have a role within resilience development. Human beings are hardwired to be social. Research has demonstrated that social connections influence how you experience pain, trauma, and adversity. Your stress response system even has components that compel you to be social, driving you to reach out to others to both offer help and ask for support (McGonigal, 2015). Nurturing your emotional and interpersonal processes, including empathy and compassion, strengthens the adaptive aspects of the stress response and improves overall resilience.

Graham (2018) highlighted two types of relational processes when she discussed ways to improve resilience: relational intelligence within, or self-compassion, and relational intelligence with others, or empathy and compassion. Developing self-compassion enables you to focus your empathy skills inward. Through self-awareness and self-acceptance, you are able to tame the brain's cons, correct cognition errors, and heal the internal dialogue that may be acting as a barrier to resiliency. A key component of self-compassion is the ability to see yourself in others and see others in yourself. This use of internal empathy helps to develop an optimistic mindset by enabling you to see yourself not as a victim of adversity, but as someone experiencing difficulties just like others experience difficulties. This, too, works to heal internal barriers to resilience and further develop this competency. I speak more about enhancing self-compassion later in this chapter.

In addition to self-compassion, nurturing empathy and compassion can result in significantly improved resilience. As I mentioned previously, our stress response is hardwired to drive us toward social interaction. In times of adversity, we are compelled to reach out to others. This taps into our empathy and compassion by allowing us to feel what others are feeling and take action. In Graham's (2018) work, she discussed using the attributes of theory of mind as a way to address and improve resilience. By understanding that you have beliefs, intentions, emotions, and knowledge that are different from another's; that he or she, similarly, has beliefs, intentions, emotions, and knowledge different from yours; and that both constructs are valid, you begin to develop an acceptance of the "other." Furthermore, through this acceptance, you can both understand another's perspective and assist another. To me, this is mature empathy and compassion. You not only can see the world from another's point of view, but also can do so while fully understanding that his or her "reality" may be different from your own. You accept this difference without judgment.

Resiliency is improved when empathy and compassion are matured. Resilience also improves when social-emotional competencies are developed. Learning emotional boundaries, developing awareness and regulation, and maturing empathy and compassion all work in harmony to improve your response to adversity and enhance your resilience.

I started this chapter with a story from my childhood that demonstrated the enmeshment that can happen when empathy is immature. This is the primary problem with empathy and why scholars like Bloom (2016) took a stand against empathy. To me, that was the wrong approach. This isn't an all-or-nothing conversation. This is about skill development and maturation. As you develop your social-emotional skills, including empathy and compassion, you improve outcomes. You improve resilience. You learn to handle life's challenges without experiencing extreme levels of distress. You begin to recognize when you are engaging in actions that don't serve you and times when your brain is working against you. As empathy and compassion mature, you are able to be a caring human without becoming emotionally distressed (due to empathy enmeshment) or experiencing compassion fatigue (due to compassion enmeshment). Tip Sheet 6: Growing Resilience provides several strategies to help you support resiliency development in your children.

TIP SHEET 6
Growing Resilience

●━━●

» Teach and practice optimism.

» Use books and media to learn about growth mindset and perseverance.

» Practice cognitive flexibility through creativity exercises. Try using some of the "spontaneous" activities from *Odyssey of the Mind* to start.

» Develop and practice mindfulness activities.

» Develop response flexibility skills.

In the next chapter, I will continue the conversation of resilience and emotional intelligence by talking about response flexibility from both an emotional and behavioral point of view.

The Nature of Self-Compassion

Compassion and empathy turned inward are commonly referred to as self-compassion. Kristen Neff (2003a, 2003b), a pioneer in the research of self-compassion, identified three major competencies involved in the development of self-compassion: self-kindness, universal humanity, and mindfulness.

Self-kindness refers to kindness toward self. Early in the chapter, I mentioned that the brain often misperceives the world, resulting in cognition errors. Often these errors involve significant levels of negative self-talk (e.g., "I'm horrible at this," "Why bother? I never succeed," etc.). I am always amazed at the depth of cruel talk people engage in internally. This lack of self-kindness often results in significant levels of emotional distress and anxiety-based thinking.

Developing self-compassion starts with changing the internal dialogue from negative to strengths-based. Chapter 5 focuses on several strategies for strengths-based practices.

In addition to negative self-talk, the willingness to practice self-care can often be reflective of your depth of self-kindness. My guess is you have no difficulty encouraging your children to practice self-care through lifestyle balance, proper food and rest, and a balanced approach to technology. But when was the last time you allowed the same for yourself? Practicing self-kindness means you also make self-care a priority. Trust me, your children will learn more about compassion for self and others if they see you modeling it!

Recognition of our common humanity is another aspect of self-compassion. This concept refers to the acceptance of a few basic truths about the human condition: We all experience pain, fear, love, and other emotions. And although we may define things somewhat differently (courtesy of theory of mind), that doesn't mean we don't have a shared experience of being human. Developing this component of self-compassion means that you have a global understanding that we all experience "stuff"—we all suffer. From that perspective, you can see yourself in another and see another in yourself.

Mindfulness is an essential aspect of self-compassion, according to Neff (2003a, 2003b). The nonjudgmental awareness and acceptance developed through mindfulness training are essential in the development of mature empathy and compassion, including self-compassion. These are the keys to nurturing emotional intelligence and resilience. Tip Sheet 7: Nurturing Self-Compassion Skills provides a variety of strategies you can use with your children. Many of these may feel difficult or strange initially. Most of us are not comfortable with self-acceptance or self-compassion. Hang in there with them. Developing this skill is essential to the overall development of the mature empathy and compassion I referred to earlier.

TIP SHEET 7
Nurturing Self-Compassion Skills

It's important to teach children to practice self-compassion skills early. Use these tips to help them show self-kindness on a regular basis:

» Teach your children about the connection between their thoughts, feelings, and actions.

» Teach your children how to listen to their inner dialogue.

» Teach your children about the brain's inner cons (e.g., catastrophic thinking) and how to beat them.

» Develop a mindfulness practice with your children.

» Teach your children to use loving kindness meditations like those offered by GoZen (https://gozen.com/love).

Whiteboard Workshop: Nurturing Self-Compassion at School

Nurturing kindness and compassion in school is nothing new. Most bully prevention programs, social-emotional learning initiatives, and school climate activities center around kindness campaigns of some form. However, most of these programs do not place emphasis on self-compassion. Often considered indulgent or inappropriate, self-compassion tends to be unnecessary to the needs of the greater community. However, self-compassion is an important aspect of emotional processes and necessary in order to mature both empathy and emotional intelligence overall (Neff, 2003a).

Schools are in a great position to teach compassion and kindness, including self-compassion. It is simple to weave the components of self-compassion within existing compassion and kindness initiatives. While teaching compassion through stories and other media, add questions about self-kindness or common humanity. When teaching mindfulness, relate it back to self-compassion. When conducting a service campaign, relate it to the universal needs of humans. All of these actions will develop self-compassion skills alongside compassion, empathy, and other social-emotional skills, and create a more positive climate for all.

Tip Sheet 8: Self-Compassion at School includes more activities that can be incorporated into a school's universal positive climate efforts.

TIP SHEET 8
Self-Compassion at School

The following activities can help to cultivate self-compassion in students (and your children at home):

- » Have students write love letters to themselves.

- » Ask students to read a story about compassion and rewrite it to focus on them.

- » Have students write affirmations to use daily.

- » Teach students to use the phrase "Even though I _____ , I still love me" whenever they are mad at themselves.

- » Ask students to engage in negative thought-busting activities like the following: Write all of the negative thoughts you have about yourself and rip up the paper. Replace the negative thoughts with positive thoughts.

Part II shifted the conversation definitions to applications, tapping into the social-emotional skills required to develop resilience and emotional intelligence. The field of positive psychology has researched these skills for the past several decades. As that research has moved from the world of academia to the mainstream, the message has shifted somewhat. Instead of remaining focused on enhancing wellness through the cultivation of social-emotional skills, people got the message that happiness and positive thinking were the only emotions worth valuing; that feeling depressed and anxious meant you did something wrong. You weren't focused on optimism. Your mindset was wrong. This has increased the feelings of anxiety and overwhelm, despite the focus on building resilience in much of today's parenting and education literature.

The truth is, no one is meant to be happy 100% of the time. Nor is anyone meant to be sad 100% of the time. Humans are endowed with a great capacity to feel. We shift in our emotions frequently. We aren't static. And this is how it should be. Learning to ride with that variance and create space in which we can choose how to engage with our emotions and the emotions of others is the key.

The next chapters build on the conversation of resilience presented in the previous pages, offering strategies to nurture emotional intelligence, develop resilience, and cultivate the space necessary for response flexibility.

Cultivating Caring Action Steps

In Part II, we move from the definitions of empathy and compassion to a deeper look at emotional intelligence competencies. Chapter 3 focused on resiliency skills, highlighting self-compassion. For your action steps, it is time to develop resiliency at home. Creating an environment that feels safe and includes predictable responses from adults, clear expectations and consequences, and opportunities to grow social-emotional skills provides the needed foundation for the development of resiliency. The following three action steps will help you begin the process of establishing a resiliency-rich home.

Empathy and Resilience

1. Take stock of your current practices and routines as a parent. Have you strengthened the relationships in your home (see Cultivating Caring Action Steps, Chapter 1)? Have you created expectations and consequences focused on empathy and compassion (see Cultivating Caring Action Steps, Chapter 2)? Have you focused on establishing and maintaining healthy boundaries (see Cultivating Caring Action Steps, Chapter 2)? Now is the time to go back and complete the action steps you may have forgotten.

2. Pay attention to the opportunities to talk about feelings that occur throughout the week. Do you make maximum use of these opportunities? If you aren't sure, hop over to Part III for specific examples of how to engage in empathy-building conversations at home. Make a list of the different opportunities and how you want to maximize conversations in the future.

3. Commit to having at least two conversations with your children about feelings, resiliency, and emotional intelligence. These don't have to be hard. Talk about a favorite book or movie. Use media they enjoy to engage in deeper conversations around grit, determination, and resiliency.

The Art of Flexibility

It seems to me that all of the focus on emotions is making us less compassionate and less resilient. Is that true?
—High school biology teacher

IN Chapter 3, I shared the story of my empathetic response to my mom's panic attack. During that period of empathy enmeshment, I experienced parallel distress to my mom. This is not a healthy response. I didn't know how to distance myself from her feelings. I wasn't able to be intentional in my emotional response, recognize my cognition errors, or reframe my thoughts. To make matters worse, I wasn't encouraged to feel my feelings in that moment. I was asked to put them aside and just move forward, yank myself out of the emotional response altogether, and pretend my experience wasn't happening.

I'm sure that was not the intentional message from the adults around me at the time. But it was certainly the message I received. And I complied. I pushed away my emotional response, something I continued to do well into my adulthood, and pushed forward. I had no understanding at the time of the impact; I didn't connect my

DOI: 10.4324/9781003238751-7

inability to manage my breathing later during an ascension test to the panic my mom experienced and the way that event still lived in my cells.

Imagine the difference if I had been encouraged to experience my emotions in the moment, emotions that were appropriate to the context (I mean, what child wouldn't be freaked out if she watched her parent in the throes of a panic attack?). Imagine if I'd been coached to process through the emotional response and intentionally choose what to do next. Imagine if I'd been taught that flexibility of emotions and behaviors were the key to growing my resilience in a healthy manner. Just imagine.

In this chapter, we will explore what it means to have emotional and behavioral flexibility, and how this enhances the development of all of our social-emotional skills, including empathy and compassion.

The Problem With the Positive Psychology Movement

Psychology is the scientific study of the human mind, emotions, and behavior. It has typically focused on ways to understand and alleviate human suffering. In 1998, while Dr. Martin E. P. Seligman was president of the American Psychological Association, a new field of psychological research evolved that shifted the perspective from suffering to wellness. Coined positive psychology, this branch of study researched the strengths and positive attributes that enable humans to thrive.

Positive psychology focuses on three central pillars: positive experiences (past, present and future), positive traits (including compassion, resilience, and integrity, among others), and positive institutions and the strengths needed for development (including tolerance, justice, and responsibility). The ideals of positive psychology have permeated society over the last 20 years, entering education, business, and criminal justice circles—and with good reason.

Research supports nurturing social-emotional wellness and developing various character traits as a way to increase personal wellness, reduce anxiety and depression, and improve outcomes (Jones et al., 2017). It is clear that focusing on growing wellness competencies works.

However, not all of the outcomes from the work of positive psychology are good. Like many other new ideas, there have been unforeseen consequences from the positive psychology movement. As this field of psychological study made its way into mainstream thinking, thought leaders, life coaches, educators, and parents interpreted the goals of happiness and positive thinking to mean that feelings of sadness and pain were to be avoided or ignored.

Scroll through the pages of life coaching and parenting advice websites or social media pages devoted to motivational sound bites, and you will find a constant push to think positively. Messages abound telling you that if you think positively, everything will be fine. You hear that negative thinking is to be banished; that sadness, disgust, and anger are the enemy. Your children receive these messages as well. All of these messages have resulted in average people feeling trapped by their emotions: If they are happy, they are good, but if they feel something else, they are doomed to bad outcomes that they, alone, could have avoided. It is no surprise that people, especially the youths of iGen, are less happy than they were a generation ago, despite the onslaught of positive psychology research and strategies in daily practice (Twenge, 2019). The constant messages on social media about being positive and happy with no counter message about the truth of the struggle humans feel from time to time has had the effect of taking only some parts of the positive psychology movement while dismissing others.

Don't misunderstand me—I believe in the tenets of positive psychology. I firmly believe in the power of optimism, the need to grow social-emotional skills, and the connection between how and what we think about and our outcomes. I also believe in a balanced approach to emotional awareness and regulation. It's time for everyone to own all of their emotions, the "positive" ones and the negative ones. It's time for our social media personas to better reflect the truth of the human condition, including the struggle to gain emotional balance that many of us feel.

This is the crux of being flexible, I believe. It is the ability to correctly identify and acknowledge your emotional states without shame or guilt, and then to choose what to do with that information. It is about claiming full agency over your thoughts, feelings, and actions. To me, this is the path to wellness. This is how you thrive.

Empathy and Emotional Flexibility
Lessons From Young Children

When I was in my undergraduate studies, I spent a lot of time learning to observe child behavior by watching preschoolers. Day after day, I sat in the back of the local preschool center and watched as boys and girls between the ages of 3 and 5 interacted. It was one of the best experiences of my life. Not only did I see child development in action, but also I was able to witness examples of raw emotion, early signs of empathy and the mechanics of mirror neurons at work.

Children under the age of 6 demonstrate the idea of emotional flexibility better than any other group. They feel whatever they feel whenever they feel it—and, boy, do they let you know! In any given hour, they may move from happy to sad, to angry to disgusted, to surprised to happy. It is a whirlwind. Uninhibited by societal norms for behavioral responses, they are free to express themselves in a purely authentic way. Although I'm not suggesting that we all should wildly express our feelings all day, every day, I do think there is something to be said for unencumbered, honest emotions.

In addition to the emotional freedoms expressed by young children, there are ideal examples of emotional contagions at work and the underpinnings of empathy. As I have mentioned, one of the neurological processes of empathy is the idea of mirror neurons. As social beings, humans have shared emotional responses to one another. If you smile, I smile. If you cry, I am likely to cry. And if you laugh, I will likely laugh.

Young children are an ideal example of this. Have you ever had a toddler cry in a room of toddlers? Within moments, the entire room is in meltdown mode. These are the raw elements of empathy at work—the toddlers are feeling into each other. In those early days of observing preschoolers, I witnessed not only the mimicry of mirror neurons, but also concern for others in pain, toddlers trying to fix classmates' "ouchies" with bandages, imaginative play that involved empathy and compassion, and prosocial behavior that encouraged others to be the best versions of themselves. It was clear to me that empathy and compassion are innate and that many of the ways adults interact with children could work against, rather than with, the natural empathy.

Let's go back to the raw emotions of toddlers. How do many adults respond when children are riding the roller coaster of their emotions? Kids are often told to "calm down," "stop crying," "buck up," and other quieting responses. The message they get is clear: It is not okay to have strong emotions. I've heard these growing up. And I've said them to others (something I am not proud of admitting). This response changes how young children interact with the world. They move from feeling and expressing their emotions, to regulating emotions based on what others think is appropriate. This is necessary in order to conform to the greater community.

But what is the price paid? Is there a way to teach children to regulate behavior more adaptively than the wild and crazy ride of emotions seen in toddlers and preschoolers? Can we learn to feel authentically without causing such high levels of distress?

I believe that the answer is yes. By changing the response to children from emotionally stunting to teaching children how to process emotions and choose responses, you can teach regulation without also teaching to ignore or discount emotions. This, in turn, helps children grow their natural empathy and compassion in a way that speeds maturity of the skill. Tip Sheet 9: Empathy Coaching provides response examples for working with young children as they learn about their emotions and behaviors. Part III also shows examples of coaching that nurtures empathy development.

TIP SHEET 9
Empathy Coaching

One of the best ways to support others in developing empathy is to model and coach empathy every day. Try these activities to cultivate and support empathy:

» Acknowledge emotions in others (e.g., "It sounds like that was hard," "Man, I bet that hurt.").

» Place no judgments on others' feelings or opinions.

» Ask how someone feels (e.g., "What a hard day! How did it make you feel?").

» Ask if you can help (e.g., "Is there anything I can do?" "What do you need?").

» Offer kindness and support (e.g., "I know it was a hard day. I'm here if you need anything.").

» Resist the urge to provide unsolicited advice, help, or "fix" the other person. Being empathetic means providing space for the other to feel without imposing your judgments on another or trying to "fix" something.

Intentional Flexibility

One of the most powerful ways to improve resilience and nurture social-emotional skills is through flexibility in thinking and response. This involves cognitive skills, emotional processes, and mindsets. Cognitive flexibility, or the ability to shift attention and thinking between concepts, is essential to developing the ability to be intentional in your responses to life. Likewise, emotional flexibility, or the ability to shift between changing emotional conditions, is also needed for response flexibility.

Graham (2013) highlighted response flexibility as one of the primary ways to improve one's resilience. By learning to reframe negative thinking (cognitive skills), reframe emotional responses (emotional processes), and adapt an optimistic and growth-oriented perspective (mindset), you can begin to take control over your responses to life's various events. You will also grow emotional intelligence and mature your empathy and compassion.

I often say that your EQ determines how much of your IQ you can use at a given time. By developing the components of emotional intelligence, you are able to activate your prefrontal cortex more readily and access your cognitive skills. Information flows more freely throughout your neurological processes. As I mentioned in Chapter 3, resiliency is the outcome of integration of those processes. The more you are able to integrate your brain, the stronger your resilience. The more you are able to support your children to integrate their neurological processes, the stronger their resilience.

This is the heart of positive psychology in my opinion—not the ignoring of adversity, but the ability to use your emotional intelligence to reflect on your experiences through a positive lens (i.e., past adversity has enabled you to experience compassion from others or develop self-reliance), embrace your character strengths (i.e., you recognize ways you are resilient or courageous) and use them to help in your areas of growth (i.e., you use your strengths in persistence to address your difficulties with temperance), and contribute positively to the planet through mature empathy and compassion. This is how we cultivate a more caring world through intentional flexibility and emotional intelligence.

Tip Sheet 10: Embracing the Positive provides strategies you can use with your children to enhance their EQ.

TIP SHEET 10
Embracing the Positive

- » Cultivate an optimistic mindset.
- » Commit to a gratitude practice every day.
- » Develop your character strengths.
- » Practice mindfulness.
- » Develop self-compassion.
- » Cultivate empathy and compassion.

Whiteboard Workshop:
Caring Starts Early

As I mentioned earlier in this chapter, the initial underpinnings of empathy can be witnessed in very young children. Preschool and transitional kindergarten are great opportunities to nurture the development of empathy and compassion through activities that grow social-emotional skills, including self- and social awareness, emotional regulation, prosocial skills, optimism, and perspective-taking.

An easy way to build awareness skills is through mindfulness. By teaching children how to quiet their thoughts and focus on the present moment, you set the stage for other social-emotional learning. Try incorporating mindful moments into the school-day routine and as part of transitioning from activities. The activities listed in Chapter 5 can also be used in a school setting to increase mindfulness practice.

Regulation in preschool-aged students begins with the development of their emotional vocabulary. Learning to label one's emotions is essential to learning to regulate one's emotions. This is particularly true with intense emotions. Label emotions—yours and your students'—throughout the day to help children learn the vocabulary needed to discuss emotional responses.

Interconnectedness is an essential part of perspective-taking and empathy development. Helping children develop their awareness of others and our shared humanity can enable the growth of empathy and compassion. Use stories to discuss how characters are interacting and the shared action-consequence that each is experiencing. The more children begin to understand the impact of their behavior and the shared experience of being human, the more empathy is nurtured.

Finally, weave kindness and strengths-focused activities into the school day. Freely give compliments, and teach children to do the same. Look for ways people are doing things right, as opposed to constantly correcting behavior. Teach students to look for each other's character strengths and call them out. Do random acts of kindness for each other and the greater school community. All of these actions naturally develop empathy and compassion skills, while also building a positive school climate for learning. Tip Sheet 11: Activities to Nurture Empathy in Young Students provides a variety of school-based ways to develop empathy in preschool.

TIP SHEET 11
Activities to Nurture Empathy in Young Students

» Develop healthy family attachments and positive relationships.

» Help your child develop an emotional vocabulary.

» Openly talk about feelings.

» Validate your child's feelings, even when you don't understand them.

» Use stories and media as a platform to talk about feelings. The Scholastic website has great suggestions for appropriate books (https://www.scholastic.com).

TIP SHEET 11, *continued*

> » Use pretend play to practice emotions and empathetic responses.
> » Model empathetic behavior.

Emotional intelligence and response flexibility are the keys to resilience and being a more caring individual. Through the development of the competencies that make up emotional intelligence, empathy and compassion mature and enable you to feel into others without judgement or distress and take action to enhance the well-being of the community as a whole. This is what it means to be caring, to contribute in positive ways to your life and the lives of others.

The world is challenging. There are many things that overwhelm our coping systems. This appears particularly true for iGen and future generations. Fine-tuning your response flexibility and nurturing your emotional intelligence have never been more vital. The tips and information here give you the resources needed to help both you and your children. Use the tips. Practice the skills. Share this information with your children. Nurturing your child's ability to care starts with nurturing your own empathy and compassion.

Cultivating Caring Action Steps

It is never too early to start developing social-emotional skills in children. This chapter focused on ways to nurture emotional flexibility and teach coping skills, as opposed to the common approach of teaching children to ignore their emotional responses. As soon as children are born, they begin to shape their responses to the world based on how others respond to them. It is important that we teach emotional flexibility, emotional awareness, and emotional regulation early. In the following action steps, you will have an opportunity to nurture social-emotional skills with your child, no matter how young.

1. Nurture your child's emotional vocabulary. Talk about feelings often and in a variety of contexts. Use the stories you read and the media you watch to define various feelings and how feeling descriptions may change based on the context.

2. If your child is very young, use pictures to label emotions. Start with basic emotions—happiness, sadness, anger, fear, disgust, and surprise. Make a booklet with pictures that show each of the emotions. Play "name that emotion" games with your children whenever possible to grow their emotional vocabulary. If your children are older, build emotional wheels that deepen their emotional vocabulary. You can play emotional detective games in which you try to come up with the most abstract emotional label for the various emotions of characters in a story. Tip Sheet 12: What's in a Name? lists a variety of emotions and synonyms. Use these to create your own.

TIP SHEET 12
What's in a Name?

» Create a dictionary of feeling words. Start with the six basic words: *joy, sadness, anger, disgust, surprise,* and *fear.*

» Ask children to draw a picture of the facial expression that indicates each word. You can also use photographs for this.

» Expand on each feeling word, adding a minimum of five synonyms for each word. Ask children to explain the differences between the words.

» Practice using the words together.

Note. Adapted from Fonseca, 2015.

---

3. Intentionally engage in conversations about feelings daily. Label emotions, talk about behavioral responses to a vari-

ety of situations, and connect feelings and behaviors to thoughts. Help your children learn to look for these connections as often as possible.

5

Mindfulness, Strengths Awareness, and Empathy

I noticed a real difference in my children's stress and behavior when I started scheduling relaxation time. I think our hurried world discourages relaxation and results in reduced emotional development.

—Blogger and mother of six

SOCIAL-EMOTIONAL learning practices, including mindfulness, strengths awareness, and compassion training continue to give rise to effectiveness debates among parents and educators. Some feel that the time needed for this learning sacrifices much needed content instruction. Others feel that learning cannot occur without a focus on the social-emotional development of children. Research is similarly conflicting, although it definitely bends toward supporting SEL in schools.

I have seen firsthand the positive impact to learning that occurs when time is spent developing emotional intelligence in children. Take Abbey, for example. She was a third-grade student in a typical classroom when I met her. She had language processing delays, significant levels of anxiety, and clear mental health concerns. She

65

DOI: 10.4324/9781003238751-8

was also one of the brightest students in her class, although most could not see her intelligence at work due to the interference of her behaviors.

Abbey struggled with her school behaviors daily. She would scream, throw tantrums, and leave the class every time she was overwhelmed. Several times a day, Abbey disrupted the class by yelling at the teacher or hiding under her desk. The classroom teacher was frustrated. The school was frustrated. The parents were frustrated. Everyone had a different idea of how best to help Abbey. Her parents felt that the teacher needed more strategies but that Abbey should stay with her class. The teacher and principal questioned whether a different environment would be more appropriate for her. I was brought in to determine the best course of action to take.

After hours of observation and working with the student, it became clear to me that her difficulties stemmed from delays in her social-emotional skill development. Working in collaboration with other specialists, we focused on building her emotional vocabulary, teaching mindfulness and strengths-based practices, and developing her empathy and compassion skills. Within a year, Abbey drastically changed. She was engaged in her classroom environment, beginning to make friends, exercising more resilience and coping strategies during challenging times, and displaying more empathy.

Not only were the changes in Abbey significant over that first year, but also the changes continued over the next several years. Yes, she still struggled with transitions. She still experienced anxiety at times and struggled to consistently communicate her needs and wants. But the focus on her emotional intelligence enabled her to express herself in different ways. Her improved EQ made it possible to utilize more of her IQ consistently in the class.

Abbey's story has been repeated throughout my professional life—with different students, adults, families, and varied needs. In every case, the answer to the difficulties the individuals faced was the same: Nurture and develop emotional intelligence using evidence-based practices, and you will improve outcomes.

In this chapter, I present three of the most common types of SEL strategies that I have found to be the most useful with a wide variety of children and needs. Mindfulness, strengths awareness, and compassion training strategies are easy to use and yield great results. Try some of the strategies throughout this chapter for yourself.

Becoming Aware

Present moment awareness, or mindfulness, as it is more commonly called, is the practice of turning your attention to the present moment completely. Through mindfulness activities, you can learn to focus your attention in the present moment, noticing your thoughts and feelings without judgement (Fonseca, 2017). Researchers have found that mindfulness practices decrease the negative impact of stress and anxiety, increase cognitive and emotional flexibility, and build resilience (Bamber & Schneider, 2016). With such a powerful tool readily available to you, it makes sense to practice mindfulness skills and teach them to your children.

Learning to be aware of the present moment begins with the simple shift from your typical noisy thoughts of the day, to whatever you are doing, feeling, and thinking in the moment. Take a minute to try a simple exercise: Close your eyes and inhale a deep breath. Visualize your thoughts as a chalkboard crowded with too many words. Picture yourself erasing all of the words until the board is blank. Once you see a blank board, attune to the present moment. What does your body feel like? What information is coming in through your senses? What thoughts are floating by? Don't try to overly label anything or problem solve what you are doing. Don't pass judgment on what you are feeling or thinking. There is no right way to start this practice. Starting by simply "being." After a few moments have passed, take a another deep breath and open your eyes. What do you notice?

If this exercise was initially difficult, that is fine. You have spent a lifetime attending to too much information at once. Most people struggle to pay attention to the present moment. It takes time to learn to find the stillness that exists inside. But it is a practice worth doing.

Try the exercise or one of the additional exercises on Tip Sheet 13: Becoming Mindful. As you and your children develop a mindfulness practice, you may begin to notice a few of the "gifts" that present moment awareness offers. You may notice that you notice your thoughts more often, the good ones and the not-so-good ones. You may feel a great sense of awareness in general. You may also notice that you have more of an ability to practice the flexibility discussed in Chapter 4.

TIP SHEET 13
Becoming Mindful

According to Niemiec (2013), mindfulness involves being aware of the present moment, focusing attention on one thing, and expanding awareness to see the gestalt. Use these activities to practive everyday mindfulness.

» **Mindful Breathing:** Close your eyes and take a deep, slow, breath through your nose. Hold briefly and exhale through your mouth. Continue with this pattern of breathing as you focus only on the breath moving through your body. As thoughts float into you mind, allow them to pass without giving them your attention. Continue for several minutes.

» **Mindful Eating:** Select an item to eat, like a strawberry or piece of banana. Take a moment to notice the color, smell, and texture of your food. As you take a bite, focus fully on the experience. What do you taste? What do you smell? Slowly chew your food, noticing the way it feels in your mouth and as you swallow. Notice how the food makes you feel, the sensations as it moves through your body. Continue until you are finished with your food.

TIP SHEET 13, *continued*

» **Mindful Walking:** Take a morning walk or hike. Focus fully on the act of walking. How does your body feel as it moves through the space? What does the air smell like? How does the wind or sun feel? Breathe deeply as you continue your walk, focusing only on the act of walking. As other thoughts come to mind, allow them to move gently through you without paying attention to them. Continue in this manner until your walk is complete.

» **Mindful Moments:** Take a moment and find a place where you can be quiet for a few minutes. I will often use my office, my car (while not driving, of course), or even the bathroom. Close your eyes and inhale a few deep breaths. Focus on your body. Where are you feeling tension? Concentrate your focus on those areas, imagining your body releasing the tightness in your muscles and fully relaxing. Do this with each area of tension until you feel fully relaxed. As thoughts float through your mind, release them without paying undue attention to them. Continue for a minute or so until your mind is clear and your body is relaxed.

Mindfulness is the key to many aspects of emotional intelligence, including resilience, empathy, and compassion (especially self-compassion). By refining your ability to slip into your present moment awareness easily, and by teaching your children to do the same, you are able to manage emotions more readily and choose your responses to the world with intent.

Strengths-Based Practices and Compassion

Another evidence-based practice that I use frequently is strengths awareness. This practice is based on the idea that all humans have a set of character strengths they use regularly, their "signature strengths." These strengths can be developed over time and used as a buffer against adversity, developing our emotional intelligence and resilience. Developing a strengths-based practice involves identifying your personal strengths, spotting the strengths in yourself and others, and using your strengths in new ways. These strategies can improve self-compassion, develop emotional intelligence, and enhance overall well-being (Niemiec, 2013).

Try this exercise with your children. Ask your children to make a list of the strengths they recognize in themselves. You can find lists of character strengths in a variety of places online. You can also take the character strengths survey on the VIA website at https://via character.org. Once your children have identified personal strengths, ask them to pay attention to the times those strengths are used over the next week. They can keep a journal of the activities. You will also keep a list of the times you see the strengths in your children. At the end of the week, talk about how and when the strengths were used. Ask what it felt like to focus on the strengths (as opposed to the common focus on shortcomings). Try this whenever your children are struggling with negative thinking or stress and anxiety. The shift of focus changes your perspective, enabling a more compassionate view. Tip Sheet 14: Strengths-Based Practices includes a variety of strategies to develop character strengths in your children.

TIP SHEET 14
Strengths-Based Practices
●——●

After identifying your most used strengths using the VIA character survey or something similar, try these exercises to make those
strengths even better:

» **Strengths Innovation:** Use your strengths in new ways.
Commit to one new way per week.

» **Seeking Strengths:** Look for strengths in others and yourself.
When you see it, call it out; everyone likes to hear about their
strengths.

» **Strengths-Based Problem Solving:** Use your strengths to
overcome life's difficulties. Actively seek ways to use your
strengths when you are challenged.

» **Strengths-Based Motivation:** When faced with something
you are avoiding, find ways that activity could tie back to your
strengths. Can you find alignment? Use this as motivation.

Compassionate Mind Training

Developed by Dr. Paul Gilbert, compassionate mind training
(CMT) is a therapeutic technique designed to use compassion, particularly self-compassion, to relieve negative feelings of shame, correct cognition errors and negative self-talk, and release anxious-like
behaviors (Gilbert & Procter, 2006). Through mindfulness activities,
visualization techniques, and relaxation strategies, people learn to
train their thinking toward kindness, empathy, and compassion.
Many of the strategies can be adopted for personal use; although
if you or your children are dealing with complex trauma, including
traumatic stress and post-traumatic stress disorder (PTSD), I would

recommend working with a highly trained professional on these techniques.

Some of the common CMT strategies include mindful breathing exercises and calming strategies. I highlighted several relaxation strategies for children in *Emotional Intensity in Gifted Students* (Fonseca, 2016) that would work well as compassionate mind training strategies, including "Breathing Colors," and "Mini-Vacations." In these strategies, you combine breathing techniques with visualization strategies to get a somatic response. Tip Sheet 15: Relaxation Strategies highlights these techniques.

TIP SHEET 15
Relaxation Strategies

» **Daily Mindfulness:** Practice mindful breathing or other mindfulness exercises daily.

» **Breathing Colors:** Take several deep breaths. On the inhalation, picture your favorite color. On the exhalation, imagine a dirty color. This is the color of the stress in your body. Continue slow steady breathing until the color you inhale matches the color you exhale.

» **Mini-Vacations:** Take a break with mental vacations whenever you are overwhelmed. Pick your vacation spot. Imagine everything about that place—how things look, how they feel, how they smell. The more vivid, the better. Immerse yourself in the vacation for 5 or 6 minutes.

» **Mental Rehearsal:** Visualize yourself successfully accomplishing your goals. Be as detailed as possible. Picture yourself engaging in each step of the goal successfully. For example, if you are preparing for a piano recital, you may picture getting ready for the recital, walking on stage, sitting on the piano bench, hearing the music in your mind, playing the

---

Another strategy, adapted from Gilbert (2010), involves visualizing the compassionate self and the compassionate other. In this exercise, you recall a time when someone was explicitly kind to you. In your mind, you call forth every sensation about the experience. As you move through the memory, you remind yourself about your strengths. The idea is to imprint the feelings you experience so you can call the emotions forward when needed. This ties into the idea of emotional and response flexibility discussed in Chapter 4, and allows you to regulate your emotions enough to engage your cognitive processes and respond flexibly to a given situation. This type of visualization could be exceptionally powerful in breaking free from anxious-like behaviors or maturing empathy skills. Tip Sheet 16: Compassion Visualization Exercises details this and other visualizations that can be used with children to develop a more compassionate thinking pattern.

TIP SHEET 16
Compassion Visualization Exercises

» **The Compassionate Vacation:** Close your eyes and take a few deep breaths. Picture your "happy" spot, the place you are most at peace. Clarify your picture using all of your senses—

the more vivid the better. Image yourself in that spot. Take a few breaths and say to yourself, "I am loved. I am at peace. I am whole." Do this anytime the day is overwhelming and you need to center your thoughts.

» **The Compassionate Friend:** Close your eyes and take a few deep breaths. Recall a moment when you comforted a friend. Replay that moment, but imagine the friend is you. Hear yourself offering comforting words and reminding you that you are worthy, you are okay. Continue with the visualization as you take deep, relaxing breaths. Do this anytime you are feeling overwhelmed and need a little pep talk.

» **Self-Care:** Close your eyes and take a few deep breaths. Recall a time when you took care of another. Picture everything you did for that other person. Imagine the same scene, but replace the person you cared for with yourself. Picture taking care of you—offering kindness and support. Imagine you helping you with chores or bringing you flowers. Feel the kindness offered—let it blanket you. Take several deep breaths and release any stresses. Do this every time you need to take a quick break from your responsibilities.

Check out Headspace and other meditation apps for specific compassion meditations that can deepen your self-compassion practice.

Whiteboard Workshop: Daily Lessons in Compassion

By now, the case for including empathy and compassion lessons into the school day is clear. Developing social-emotional skills increases academic performance, decreases incidences of bullying and violence, and promotes a positive school climate (Graham, 2018; Willis, 2018). Weaving lessons that promote empathy and compassion into the curriculum does not need to be difficult. The following suggestions are easy ways to incorporate activities in a variety of content areas at school:

- Use bibliotherapy to enhance social-emotional development: Books are a fantastic source for compassion and empathy training in school. Pick books that show a variety of emotions and responses, or specific emotional themes. Engage students in conversations about the text, probing their emotional reactions and thoughts about the events in the story. Building on curriculum requirements around reading and literature analysis, include activities that delve into the emotional and social contexts of the stories to nurture social-emotional development.
- Use test-taking routines and strategies to develop a healthy mindset: Students take many tests throughout their academic career. Why not use test prep time to grow grit and develop a growth mindset? Teach students how to use positive thinking to get "unstuck" when struggling with a test question. Teach breathing and mindfulness strategies to regulate emotions. Teach visualization techniques to develop optimism, perseverance, and grit.
- Use community circles to build relationships and develop empathy: Community circles are becoming a common practice in schools and are used to develop safe and caring environments for learning. Use community circles to build trust and respect with students. Community-building questions

75

can be used to teach interconnectedness, emotional regulation, self-awareness, prosocial skills, and more.

As you embed social-emotional learning into the activities you do throughout the school day, students get opportunities to develop competencies, practice skills, and increase emotional intelligence.

Developing empathy and compassion is possible. Creating a mindfulness practice that enables you to pause during a crisis, become present, tune into your needs and the needs of others, and take action to help yourself and others is not only possible, but necessary. Tapping into your strengths as you help others can give you the motivation you need to move through adversity. It is worth the time to develop these skills. Increasing your resilience and supporting the emotional intelligence of your children will result in a more caring home, and a more caring world.

Use the tips sprinkled throughout this chapter and the book. Take note of what works within your household and use them again. In Part III, you will see empathy in action through a variety of role-play scenarios designed to help you nurture your caring child through the day, every day.

Cultivating Caring Action Steps

Developing social-emotional learning skills, including empathy and compassion, isn't something we should only do within the school setting. The home is a primary environment for children. Incorporating mindfulness, strengths awareness, and empathy development into the daily routine at home is an important way to nurture emotional intelligence in our children. Chapter 5 focused on how social-emotional skill development can increase empathy and compassion in children. Your action steps take the information into the home and into daily use. The following three items listed focus on ways to incorporate some of the strategies used in schools within the home environment:

Mindfulness, Strengths Awareness, and Empathy

1. Incorporate intentional moments for relaxation and present moment awareness into your children's daily routine. Schedule relaxation before bedtime or a form of mindfulness as children transition from school to home. By incorporating this into the schedule, children develop a habit of relaxation and present moment awareness. These strategies intentionally build self-awareness and emotional regulation.

2. Ask children to list their character strengths. You can use the VIA survey mentioned in the chapter or a simple list of common character strengths. Use the list to help children find motivation (by aligning a task to their strengths), find the upside of adversity, or navigate stressful situations. Make it an annual practice to review their list and adjust as needed.

3. Practice self-compassion. Yes, compassion for oneself. Parenting can be challenging. Some days it is hard to remember to show love and kindness to yourself. Your obligations to your children and the other household roles you have often leave little time for you. However, if you continually put the needs of others first, you will leave yourself empty. The emptiness can easily turn to resentment—not a good emotion for parenting. Take time today to schedule some self-care. Take a walk, lounge in a bubble bath, read a book, go to the mall alone—all of these activities may give you just enough time to regroup and breathe. Tip Sheet 17: The Practice of Self-Compassion has a variety of things you can do to show a little kindness to yourself. Intentionally engaging in self-compassion practices models good boundaries and emotional balance for your children.

TIP SHEET 17
The Practice of Self-Compassion

- » Nurture resilience and emotional intelligence competencies.
- » Set and maintain healthy boundaries.
- » Practice kind assertiveness.
- » Commit to completing random acts of kindness weekly.
- » Take yourself out on a date.
- » Engage in self-compassion meditations.
- » Pay attention to self-talk and change the script on negative talk.

Empathy in Action

THE focus of *The Caring Child* has been to provide you, the parent, with the knowledge and strategies you need to best support your child with his or her emotional development. Knowledge of what to do and why you should do it is not always enough. Sometimes you just need someone to show you how to put the various strategies in action. Part III was written to provide you with examples of how the various recommendations and strategies work in real life.

Using a role-play format, I've pulled from more than 20 years of experience working with families to provide a variety of scenarios found in home, school, and community settings. Each role-play provides real-world examples of conversations between children and adults and coaching strategies to transform the everyday moments into powerful empathy and compassion building tools.

 DOI: 10.4324/9781003238751-9

6

Empathy in the Home

I'd like to think empathy can be taught. I know it is something we focus on in our family.

—Homeschooling mother of two

TEACHING empathy begins at home. Doing chores, watching a movie together, game night—these events all present opportunities to model empathy and compassion, discuss what these skills mean in the world, and teach children how to be more caring. It is essential for parents to take advantage of the naturally occurring moments within the day—to view every interaction with your children as teachable moments not to be squandered away through inaction or distraction. This requires that you are present as a parent, that you aren't distracted by your technology. I know that it can be tough. Parents are busy. Work and life pressures often bring a desire for distraction and distance. Although I firmly believe that parents need to prioritize their self-care, it is equally important that you remain engaged enough to be able to thoughtfully respond to the various things that occur at home within the day or week and look for oppor-

DOI: 10.4324/9781003238751-10

tunities to model or talk about empathy and compassion. It is the best way to incorporate these skills into a child's daily life.

In the following scenarios, I've presented examples of how to talk with our children in ways that develop emotional intelligence. The examples demonstrate empathy, compassion, and the social-emotional skills necessary for our children.

Siblings

"Stop taking my clothes!"
"I didn't take your clothes. They're ugly."
"You did take them. Mom, Sammy keeps taking my stuff."
"Did not."
"Did so."

We all know the scene—your children bickering over clothes early in the morning. We're also all familiar with the arguments that ensue after dinner when it's time to clean up or the fights over screen time and similar things. Sibling disagreements are one of the most discussed things during parent coaching and with good reason. But these moments don't need to turn into a reoccurring nightmare. In fact, these are perfect opportunities to teach perspective-taking, empathy, and emotional flexibility.

Scenario

Jhanna and Jessica are sisters born 3 years apart. For most of their childhood, they got along well, engaging in minor arguments over clothes and bathroom time. Every yelling match was quickly resolved, and they returned to being each other's best friend and closest ally. Until puberty. Things changed fast then. Now they can barely spend 5 minutes together without World War III breaking out.

Empathy in the Home

Initial Dialogue

In this scenario, Jhanna and Jessica come home from school angry. As they bound through the door, their voices elevated, you know it's going to be a rough night.

Jhanna:	You are such a brat, Jessica. I can't believe you did that to me.
Jessica:	Me? What about you? You're the one that told everyone I failed my test.
Jhanna:	Go ahead and blame me. That's what you always do.
Mom:	Girls, lower your voices. What's going on?
Jessica:	(*Still yelling*) Jhanna told the whole school that I'm stupid. Everyone laughed at me at lunch.
Jhanna:	You're such a stupid liar. Tell Mom what you did to me!
Mom:	Whoa, let's not say "stupid." Jessica, what did you do to Jhanna?
Jessica:	It wasn't a big deal. I just told her friends that she wasn't allowed to go to parties yet. It wasn't a lie. She's not.
Jhanna:	But you didn't have to say anything. You should've stayed out of my conversation.
Jessica:	And you shouldn't have told everyone about my test. You are always so mean.
Jhanna:	I didn't lie either. You did fail. Besides, no one cares about your stupid math test anyway.
Mom:	Jhanna, stop. You know your sister cares a lot about her grades. You shouldn't say anything.
Jhanna:	Take her side; you always do.
Mom:	I'm not taking anyone's side.

> *Jhanna:* Yes, you are. Whatever, I know she's the "favorite." *(Jhanna storms out of the room.)*
>
> *Mom:* Come back here. This isn't done. *(Jhanna's door slams.)* Jessica, go to your room. We'll talk about this later.

Analysis of Dialogue

In this scenario, both girls have broken trust with each other and used embarrassing truths to cause emotional or social pain. It was a perfect opportunity to talk about the problem openly to help both girls see from the other's perspectives. Instead, the conversation escalated, with at least one of the children not feeling heard and eventually leaving the room.

Let's examine the dialogue closely to see where a different response could have changed the conversation completely:

> *Jhanna:* You are such a brat, Jessica. I can't believe you did that to me.
>
> *Jessica:* Me? What about you? You're the one that told everyone I failed my test.
>
> *Jhanna:* Go ahead and blame me. That's what you always do.
>
> *Mom:* Girls, lower your voices. What's going on?

The parent's first focus is on behavior, specifically the yelling. Although it is vital to correct behavioral missteps, by asking the girls to lower their voices first, the parent is blocking communication. This action implies that yelling behavior is more important than why the children are yelling in the first place.

> *Jessica:* *(Still yelling)* Jhanna told the whole school that I'm stupid. Everyone laughed at me at lunch.

Empathy in the Home

> *Jhanna:* You're such a stupid liar. Tell Mom what you did to me!
>
> *Mom:* Whoa, let's not say "stupid." Jessica, what did you do to Jhanna?

Again, the focus is on the behavior instead of the emotions and thoughts behind the action. Further, the parent has focused most of her responses on one particular child. Both of these responses are silencing to that child.

> *Jessica:* It wasn't a big deal. I just told her friends that she wasn't allowed to go to parties yet. It wasn't a lie. She's not.
>
> *Jhanna:* But you didn't have to say anything. You should've stayed out of my conversation.
>
> *Jessica:* And you shouldn't have told everyone about my test. You are always so mean.
>
> *Jhanna:* I didn't lie either. You did fail. Besides, no one cares about your stupid math test anyway.

The conversation is running away from the parent and escalating. This has only one end—more conflict.

> *Mom:* Jhanna, stop. You know your sister cares a lot about her grades. You shouldn't say anything.
>
> *Jhanna:* Take her side; you always do.
>
> *Mom:* I'm not taking anyone's side.

The argument now shifts from a dispute between the girls to a disagreement between one girl and the parent. This serves as a distraction from the actual issue and triggers the parent in the process.

Jhanna: Yes. you are. Whatever, I know she's the "favorite." *(Jhanna storms out of the room.)*

Mom: Come back here. This isn't done. *(Jhanna's door slams.)* Jessica, go to your room. We'll talk about this later.

At this point, the conversation is over, and both Jhanna and Mom are frustrated. Neither Jhanna's nor Jessica's concerns are heard or resolved. Everyone is emotionally charged and frustrated.

New Dialogue Using Coaching Strategies

Using empathy-oriented conversation techniques and previously discussed emotional intelligence building strategies, let's look at how this dialogue could be improved and the scenario changed:

Jhanna: You are such a brat, Jessica. I can't believe you did that to me.

Jessica: Me? What about you? You're the one that told everyone I failed my test.

Jhanna: Go ahead and blame me. That's what you always do.

Mom: Girls? It sounds like you are both angry. Let's take a moment to breathe and figure out what happened.

Mom has labeled the emotions she sees and offered a strategy to allow the girls to re-engage the thinking part of their brains before engaging in a conversation. She has cued the girls to her expectation that they will manage their behavioral responses, while still acknowledging their emotions.

Jessica: *(Takes a deep breath before speaking)* Jhanna told the whole school that I'm stupid. Everyone laughed at me at lunch.

Empathy in the Home

> *Mom:* Did she really say you were "stupid"? Or did she say something else?

By asking for clarification in this way, and before the other child can react to the words, the parent is asking the child to reflect on her communication and be clearer. This will help in the conversation to follow.

> *Jessica:* She didn't say "stupid." She said I failed my test. But it made me feel stupid. And everyone laughed at me.
>
> *Jhanna:* Tell Mom what you did to me! It was way worse.
>
> *Mom:* I want to hear the whole story, Jhanna. But first I have more questions. Jessica, I'm sure it hurt when other people laughed at you. What did you do?
>
> *Jessica:* When they laughed? I went to the library. I can't be out there when the kids are like that. It's too hard.
>
> *Mom:* I understand that. And did you talk to Jhanna about it?
>
> *Jhanna:* No. She did something worse!
>
> *Mom:* Let Jessica tell me. I promise I want to hear your side as well. Jessica?

At this point, the parent is clearly in control of the conversation. She is ignoring the minor behaviors while maintaining communication, validating the feelings and creating a safe environment in which to talk about the event.

> *Jessica:* I . . . I . . . No, I didn't talk to Jhanna. I was too mad. I just said something to her friends. I wanted to make her feel as bad as she made me feel.
>
> *Mom:* I see. And did it work? Did you make her feel bad?
>
> *Jessica:* Yes.

The Caring Child

Mom: Did it make you feel better?

Jessica: Not really.

Mom: Hmm. Let's talk more about that in a minute. Jhanna, your turn. What did your sister say to your friends?

Using reflection and guided questions, the parent is able to help Jessica look at her behavior more closely and through an empathy lens. The parent stays focused on one child before engaging the second half of the story. This allows for a fuller picture of what occurred. With conflict, there is often a series of events that led to the larger explosion. By looking at each part, not only will the parent get a clearer picture of what actually transpired, but also there are often several opportunities for empathy development.

Let's see how the conversation ends.

Jhanna: Jessica told everyone that I can't go out with them—that you and Dad are super strict and I'm always in trouble and grounded.

Mom: How did that make you feel?

Jhanna: Embarrassed. She made it sound like I'm an irresponsible delinquent or something.

Mom: Did your friends say anything?

Jhanna: No. Most of them have younger siblings. They get it.

Mom: Okay. Did you explain to your sister how you felt?

Jhanna: What's the point? She never listens.

Mom: I think the point is to help her see your perspective— just like you could try to see her perspective on the math test situation.

From here, the parent can coach the kids to see each other's perspective, empathize with each other's feelings, and find a solution to move forward. This type of dialogue takes longer and requires more sustained focus from the parent, but it can result in true social-emotional growth and rebuild some broken trust. Both girls get an opportunity to be heard and to listen. Both get to be part of a solution.

Screen Time

Conflict over screen time rules has become one of the most common issues in my parent coaching practice over the past few years. Concern over the amount of time, enforcing household rules, and what to do when rules are violated are regular conversations—and with good reason. As discussed in Chapter 1, screen time use is linked to many mental health concerns, including increases in anxiety and depression. Furthermore, screen time is addictive, with a similar neurological impact as heroin and cocaine use. Managing screen time with our children is important. But conflict isn't always a bad thing. There is great potential for increased empathy and the potential to further teach social-emotional skills with every conversation.

In this scenario, we will examine how to use screen time rule violations as an opportunity to practice emotional flexibility and empathy skills.

Scenario

Ben is a 10-year-old child engrossed with *Minecraft*. He loves building worlds and playing with his friends. His household rules around *Minecraft* are simple:

- Screen time is allowed after homework and before 8 p.m.
- Screen time is allowed after chores.
- Screen time rules are subject to change whenever parents deem necessary.

The Caring Child

Initial Dialogue

In this scenario, Ben has been sneaking screen time every night. His parents discover the rule violation from another parent.

Dad: Ben, Ms. Jacobson told me that she overheard you bragging about sneaking time on Minecraft late each night. Is this true?

Ben: I wouldn't do that, Dad. You know that.

Dad: I would like to think that she is mistaken. But she is certain about what she heard. I will ask again. Are you sneaking screen time without permission?

Ben: (He shifts in his seat and looks down, silent.)

Dad: I expect an answer, Ben.

Ben: It's not a big deal. Everyone else gets to play Minecraft at night. Why can't I? It's not fair.

Dad: You know the rules, Ben.

Ben: They're stupid rules. I don't see why it matters when I play. Isn't Minecraft supposed to be educational? Isn't it good that I want to play?

Dad: It doesn't matter. The rule is that all screen time happens before 8. You broke the rule. And you lied. Mom and I have no choice but to take away all screen time for a week.

Ben: What? That's not fair. I hate this place and those rules. (Ben storms off to his bedroom.)

Analysis of Dialogue

In this scenario, Ben has been caught in a lie and breaking a household rule. Although the consequence is wholly appropriate and the conversation is generally fine, there are some opportunities for empathy development that have been missed.

Let's examine the dialogue closely to see where opportunities for skill development may occur.

Dad: Ben, Ms. Jacobson told me that she overheard you bragging about sneaking time on Minecraft late each night. Is this true?

Ben: I wouldn't do that, Dad. You know that.

Dad: I would like to think that she is mistaken. But she is certain about what she heard. I will ask again. Are you sneaking screen time without permission?

On the surface, this is a great conversation. But there is an opportunity for empathy modeling that is missed when the dad focuses on the accuracy of Ben's statement instead of what Ben is likely feeling.

Ben: (He shifts in his seat and looks down, silent.)

Dad: I expect an answer, Ben.

Ben: It's not a big deal. Everyone else gets to play Minecraft at night. Why can't I? It's not fair.

Dad: You know the rules, Ben.

The focus is squarely on the rule violation. Although this is appropriate, there are a few more missed opportunities to model empathy and teach perspective. Further, it is clear that the dad is not interested in a conversation as much as confirmation of the rule violation.

Ben: They're stupid rules. I don't see why it matters when I play. Isn't Minecraft supposed to be educational? Isn't it good that I want to play?

> *Dad:* It doesn't matter. The rule is that all screen time hap-
> pens before 8. You broke the rule. And you lied. Mom
> and I have no choice but to take away all screen time for
> a week.

The conversation is over. There is no interest in hearing the child's perspective or in in teaching empathy or emotional skills, and the result of the lockdown of communication is Ben's reaction below.

> *Ben:* What? That's not fair. I hate this place and those rules.
> *(Ben storms off to his bedroom.)*

Although Ben's behavior is predictable and expected, a differ-ent outcome may have been achieved with a different approach and response from Dad.

New Dialogue Using Coaching Strategies

Now that the opportunities for empathy development have been pinpointed, let's take a look at how the conversation is improved with empathy-building techniques woven in.

> *Dad:* Ben, I heard sometime troubling today. Ms. Jacobson
> told Mom and I that you have been playing Minecraft
> after bedtime. Is this true?
>
> *Ben:* I wouldn't do that, Dad. You know that.
>
> *Dad:* I do believe that you know the rules and usually respect
> them. I also know that playing Minecraft is super fun
> and something you really enjoy doing. Is it possible that
> you have been sneaking in the screen time, even though
> you know you are breaking a rule?

Empathy in the Home

Dad validates his son's statement while also providing reasons why the behavior may have occurred. This creates a caring space for Ben to admit what he did when Dad asks again.

Ben: *(He shifts in his seat and looks down, silent.)*

Dad: It can be really scary to admit when you've broken a rule. Are you feeling scared right now?

Dad labels the potential feeling he sees in his son and shifts the question to the feelings. He is again modeling empathy and compassion by providing a safe and caring environment in which Ben can own his behavior.

Ben: *(He nods but remains silent.)*

Dad: Have you been playing Minecraft after bedtime?

Ben: *(He nods again.)*

Dad: Can you tell me why you chose to break the rules?

Ben: I wasn't thinking about that. I just created a new game and needed to play it. So, I did.

Dad: What does "needed to play it" mean?

Ben: I had to. I knew I shouldn't, but I had to anyway.

Dad: Did it feel like nothing else mattered right in that moment?

Ben: Yeah.

Dad: I understand. Do you remember when we talked about screen time being addicting?

Ben has admitted what he did, and a conversation around tech addiction can now happen with real-life examples. Ben gets an opportunity to fully understand why his behavior was concerning to his parents. This is not to say there should not also be a consequence for the rule violation. But consequences alone will not change behavior in the long-term. Growing social-emotional skills, including empathy and compassion, is a better way to change behavior.

Let's see how the conversation about the consequence can unfold.

> Dad: Although I do understand how hard it is to resist things we feel compelled to do, there is a household rule about screen time, right?
>
> Ben: Yes, there is.
>
> Dad: And you did violate the rule, yes?
>
> Ben: I did.
>
> Dad: And you bragged about "getting away with it" to your friend, yes?
>
> Ben: Yes.
>
> Dad: So, what do you think would be a fair consequence for the rule violation and the bragging?
>
> Ben: Hmm. A month with no screen time at all?
>
> Dad: A month sounds extreme to me. Do you think you need a month without Minecraft to reduce your need for it?

Dad and Ben can reach a reasonable consequence, something that meets the needs of both the parent and the child. The door is also open for continued conversation around the boasting about inappropriate behavior. Through the subtle changes in language and tone, this conversation has become a powerful tool to further develop social-emotional skills. Review the action items in Chapter 1 for more ideas around setting screen time expectations.

Increasing Independence

It happens to every parent sooner or later, the time when your child pushes the limits and asks for more independence. He or she begins rejecting parental involvement. It may be subtle—walking out of the room when on the phone, or asking you to do school drop offs a little farther away. Or it may come in a rush—sneaking out or lying about where he or she has been. No matter how it manifests, the push for independence is an important developmental jump for our children.

As I discussed in Chapter 1, this generation of children seeks independence a little later than previous generations. It may be that you are ready for your child to have a little more independence before your child expresses interest. Regardless of who initiates the change, growing up and increasing independence and responsibility are times when conflict can arise. They are also events rife with opportunities to grow social-emotional learning skills and model empathy and compassion.

In this scenario, a mother and daughter wrestle with increased independence involving friends, the movies, and parental supervision.

Scenario

Lizzie is not like many of her friends. She enjoys being independent, going out with friends, and taking control of her life. Her mother doesn't enjoy it as much. She recognizes the dangers in the world. Stories of girls being kidnapped at the mall, taken advantage of on the way to school, and hurt by neighbors have caused her to be cautious. Too cautious. She seldom allows Lizzie to go to the movies without adult supervision or hang out with friends unless a parent is with her all of the time.

The Caring Child

Initial Dialogue

Now that Lizzie is in eighth grade, she wants to be able to go to the movies without her mom. She also wants to go bowling or shopping at the mall without parental supervision. In short, she wants more freedom and is determined to get it.

Lizzie: Becky invited me to the movies on Friday. Can I go?

Mom: I don't know. Who's going to be there?

Lizzie: Just Becky and Andi.

Mom: What about a parent?

Lizzie: I don't think so. Parents usually don't like to watch the same movies. So can I go?

Mom: You know I really don't like you going to the mall without a parent.

Lizzie: Mom, I'm 13, not 5. Why can't I just go with my friends? It's not like we are going to do anything other than see a movie.

Mom: It's not safe. I really think you should have a parent there. How about I go with you?

Lizzie: Mom, no! I can't believe you. You're always hovering.

Mom: Don't talk to me like that. You know why I get concerned. Just yesterday—

Lizzie: Stop, Mom. Just stop. Just because you're afraid of everything doesn't mean I have to be. All I want is to go to the movies with Becky. That's all.

Mom: If you aren't going to respect my wishes, then I have to say "no." You can't go.

Lizzie: I can't believe you. Fine. Whatever. (*She stomps off to her room.*)

Empathy in the Home

Analysis of Dialogue

In this scenario, Lizzie and her mom both make valid points. But in an effort to be heard, neither listens to the other or models empathy. Let's take a look at the missed opportunities for deeper conversations and understanding in the dialogue.

Lizzie: Becky invited me to the movies on Friday. Can I go?

Mom: I don't know. Who's going to be there?

Lizzie: Just Becky and Andi.

Mom: What about a parent?

Lizzie: I don't think so. Parents usually don't like to watch the same movies. So can I go?

Mom: You know I really don't like you going to the mall without a parent.

Although this is an appropriate conversation on the surface, there are multiple missed opportunities to reflect on emotion and empathy, as well as deepen the parent-child connection.

Lizzie: Mom, I'm 13, not 5. Why can't I just go with my friends? It's not like we are going to do anything other than see a movie.

Mom: It's not safe. I really think you should have a parent there. How about I go with you?

Lizzie: Mom, no! I can't believe you. You're always hovering.

Mom is definitely trying to find a solution that works, but she is not hearing Lizzie's need for independence. This results in a quick deterioration of the conversation.

Mom: Don't talk to me like that. You know why I get concerned. Just yesterday—

Lizzie: Stop, Mom. Just stop. Just because you're afraid of everything doesn't mean I have to be. All I want is to go to the movies with Becky. That's all.

At this point, no one is listening. Mom is feeling unheard and disrespected. So is Lizzie.

Mom: If you aren't going to respect my wishes, then I have to say "no." You can't go.

Lizzie: I can't believe you. Fine. Whatever. *(She stomps off to her room.)*

The conversation ends on a sour note. Neither participant understands nor empathizes with the other. Everyone is very fixated on their point of view. No one leaves the conversation satisfied.

New Dialogue Using Coaching Strategies

Using some of the strategies from earlier sections of the book, let's see how the conversation can be transformed into something more meaningful with a better outcome:

Lizzie: Becky invited me to the movies on Friday. Can I go?

Mom: That sounds fun. Are you excited?

Lizzie: Totally. Can I go?

Mom: I need a little more information before I can say "yes."

Empathy in the Home

In this new beginning to the conversation, Mom is coming from an empathetic perspective from the start. She also expresses her need (more information) and her expected response (a potential "yes").

Lizzie:　Sure. What do you need to know?

Mom:　The usual information: Where is the movie playing, what time are you going and when will you return, who are you going with? You know, typical parent stuff! (*By injecting a little humor, Mom is keeping the mood light while still getting the information she needs. She is also setting a behavioral expectation for future requests.*)

Lizzie:　We want to see the new Cole Sprouse movie at the mall. Becky's mom said she'd take Becky, Andi, and I there after school and pick us up after the movie. I'd be home after that. Cool? Can I go?

Mom has already gotten more details than the previous version of the conversation. And Lizzie and Mom are still open in their communication patterns because no one is feeling threatened or unheard.

Mom:　It sounds like Becky's mom is just doing pick-up and drop-off. Is that correct?

Lizzie:　Yep.

Mom:　I'll be honest, Lizzie, I have a little concern about allowing you to go to the mall and the movies without a parent. We haven't really allowed that previously. Do you feel ready for that level of independence?

Mom is approaching her concerns from a much different place in this example. She is focused on Lizzie's growth and development and allowing her to have agency in the decision. She is empathetic and seeking to understand Lizzie instead of reacting to fear.

The Caring Child

> *Lizzie:* I think I'm ready. I know that I need to stay at the movies and with my friends. Kids my age do this all of the time, Mom.
>
> *Mom:* You sound excited to take on more independence.
>
> *Lizzie:* I am.
>
> *Mom:* Do you understand my reluctance . . . my concerns?
>
> *Lizzie:* I think so. It's a mom thing, right? You're worried that something will happen to me.

In this section, both Lizzie and her mom are able to have an honest conversation and express their perspectives. Both parties share empathy and respect for each other's points of view. This is the beginning of many important conversations as Lizzie enters adolescence. Let's see how the conversation ends.

> *Mom:* Yes, it is a mom thing. So what can we do to allow you the freedom you want—an appropriate thing to ask for at your age—and me to feel that you will be safe from harm? *(Mom has an idea of what she would like to happen, but she is giving Lizzie agency to allow for skill practice in additional areas of social-emotional development.)*
>
> *Lizzie:* What if I checked in throughout the time? Like if I texted you when we got there, when the movie started, and when we were heading home? Could we try that, please? This is really important to me, Mom.
>
> *Mom:* Okay. We can try. But if I don't feel like you are safe, I will pick you up myself, okay?
>
> *Lizzie:* Okay.

Although Mom did not get exactly what she wanted—parental supervision forever for her daughter—she was able to work out an appropriate solution that allowed Lizzie to begin the all-important process of growing her decision-making skills and independence. By modeling empathy, Mom was able to hear her daughter's wishes and express her own concerns. This was a much healthier and productive conversation for everyone involved. As Lizzie enters adolescence, there will be many difficult conversations ahead. This example sets the tone for future conversations and helps develop emotional flexibility and emotional intelligence. See Tip Sheet 18: Conversation Strategies to Develop Empathy for more information.

TIP SHEET 18
Conversation Strategies to Develop Empathy

- » Practice active listening techniques.
- » Reflect the emotions behind the words whenever possible.
- » When in doubt, ask. Assume nothing.
- » Tone and voice matter.
- » Focus on modeling compassion for your child.
- » Be ready for roadblocks:
  - › Typical child roadblocks include yelling, whining, and ignoring.
  - › Typical parental roadblocks include threatening, judging, and shaming.

Divorce

Although the divorce rate has been decreasing over the past few decades, nearly 50% of marriages continue to end in divorce. When the marriage involves children, divorce can result in complicated custody arrangements and split households. For the parents, this can mean frustration and anger as they try to work through differences in parenting structure, household rules, and conflict within the relationships. For the children, there are often myriad emotional reactions. They may feel pain over the loss of their family structure, confusion over mixed parental feelings and messages within the two households, and even relief that daily stress is over.

Adjustment to the new family reality after a divorce can be positive if everyone approaches the situation from a place of empathy and compassion. Yes, there will be difficult times. But empathy and compassion can enable every person to embrace the other perspectives and work together toward healthier relationships.

In this scenario, divorced parents must learn how to communicate in order to help their child with a school problem.

Scenario

Ten-year-old Jake's parents have been divorced for 3 years. Since that time, Jake has spent his time split between two very different households. Every other Monday, Jake goes to his father's new condo and stays for a week. At Dad's house, the rules are laid-back. Jake is expected to do his homework and stay out of trouble at school, but Dad never checks to make sure these things are completed. They spend most nights playing video games or going to the skate park. Jake enjoys the time a lot.

When Jake isn't with Dad, he lives in the family home with Mom and his grandmother. Like Dad, Jake's Mom expects homework to be completed and behavior to be appropriate in school and at home. But unlike Dad, Mom checks on the homework and school behavior often. There is little time for games at Mom's house. Instead, time is spent on homework or chores. Any free time is spent in the backyard or at a neighbor's house playing with friends. Jake's Mom and Dad seldom talk and are generally unaware of the differences between the two households.

Jake doesn't mind the two households. In fact, he often uses his parent's lack of communication to his advantage, hiding problems at school and poor grades whenever possible.

Empathy in the Home

Initial Dialogue

One day, Jake's mom gets a call from school on her "off" week. Although she tries to pass the call off to Dad, the school insists on making her aware of growing problems with Jake's schoolwork. After she gets off the phone, she calls Jake's dad at work and explains that Jake is failing three classes and has been in many altercations at school this year. They decide to speak with him together to find out what is happening.

Mom: Jake, your father and I are very disappointed in your grades and school behavior. What do you have to say about everything?

Jake: What do you mean?

Mom: Don't be flippant with me. You know what I mean. You are failing three classes and have been to the principal's office repeatedly. Worse, you've hidden this from us both.

Jake: I honestly don't know what you mean.

Dad: *(In a firm and frustrated tone)* Stop it, Jake. You've lied to your mom and me. You hide your schoolwork from us and forged my signature on your suspension slips.

Jake: You never asked me about my schoolwork, Dad.

Mom: Don't blame your father. He trusted you. So did I.

Jake: *(He crosses him arms and looks at the ground.)*

Dad: Well? What do you have to say for yourself?

Jake: *(He says silent.)*

Mom: This is serious, honey. We expect an answer from you.

Jake: No, you don't. You're both so busy with your own lives that you don't care about mine. School sucks. It's always sucked. The work is hard, the kids suck, and I hate it.

Dad: That's no excuse. You know the rules. Do your work, try hard, and stay out of trouble. It's not complicated.

Jake: For you, maybe. But it's really hard for me. It always has been. You guys just never notice.

Dad: Enough. I don't want to hear excuses or have you shift blame. You are responsible for your actions. Your mother and I agree that you are grounded. No more skate park. No video games. You are getting a tutor to help you, and you'll have extra chores.

Jake: What? That's so unfair. I can get my grades up. You don't have to ground me.

Mom: Clearly, we do. And don't think you'll be fooling either of us anymore. Your teachers are e-mailing the assignments to both of us, and we'll be checking on your work every night.

Jake: Great. Like prison.

Dad: Prison is where you're headed if you keep up this nonsense. Now get your work out and finish your homework. You will need to make up all missing work as well. This behavior ends. Now.

Jake: (He storms off, mumbling under his breath.)

Analysis of Dialogue

In this scenario, Jake's parents are very angry and disappointed in Jake's behavior. Jake is trying to shift blame, age-normal behavior for a 10-year-old boy. Although the consequence is appropriate for this situation, there is no empathy development or social-emotional skill strengthening during the conversation. Neither side is interested in conversation; Jake and his parents are only interested in getting their points across and establishing some autonomy over the events.

Let's examine the dialogue more closely and see where opportunities to deepen relationships and practice social-emotional learning skills were missed.

Mom: Jake, your father and I are very disappointed in your grades and school behavior. What do you have to say about everything?

Jake: What do you mean?

Mom: Don't be flippant with me. You know what I mean. You are failing three classes and have been to the principal's office repeatedly. Worse, you've hidden this from us both.

Immediately the parent is communicating that she is not interested in Jake's point of view. This is a very authoritative conversation, and the parents are very much in charge. Although this is necessary at times, opportunities to build empathy and model compassion are unavailable with this type of approach.

Jake: I honestly don't know what you mean.

Dad: (*In a firm and frustrated tone*) Stop it, Jake. You've lied to your mom and me. You hide your schoolwork from us and forged my signature on your suspension slips.

Jake: You never asked me about my schoolwork, Dad.

Mom: Don't blame your father. He trusted you. So did I.

Feeling threatened, Jake is responding in a way that further angers his parents. This is a typical response, although not appropriate. For Jake to learn other ways to respond, the parents will also need to respond differently and model an empathetic approach.

The Caring Child

Jake: *(He crosses him arms and looks at the ground.)*

Dad: Well? What do you have to say for yourself?

Jake: *(He stays silent.)*

Mom: This is serious, honey. We expect an answer from you.

At this point, Jake has completely shut down. He is feeling unheard and victimized. From this position, he will struggle to accept responsibility for his behaviors. Further, when a similar situation arises, it is reasonable to assume he could respond in a similar manner because he is not learning new response patterns or additional social-emotional skills.

Jake: No, you don't. You're both so busy with your own lives that you don't care about mine. School sucks. It's always sucked. The work is hard, the kids suck, and I hate it.

Dad: That's no excuse. You know the rules. Do your work, try hard, and stay out of trouble. It's not complicated.

Jake: For you maybe. But it's really hard for me. It always has been. You guys just never notice.

Dad: Enough. I don't want to hear excuses or have you shift blame. You are responsible for your actions. Your mother and I agree that you are grounded. No more skate park. No video games. You are getting a tutor to help you, and you'll have extra chores.

In the heat of the moment, Jake wears down and tells his parents what he is feeling. I doubt he intended to share this information, but he did. Rather than hear the concern, however, his parents view the information as further victimization, and the moment to show empathy and compassion is lost. The parents again shut down communication in favor of exerting control over the conversation. This is not a willful attempt to silence Jake, but a nonempathetic response.

Jake: What? That's so unfair. I can get my grades up. You don't have to ground me.

Mom: Clearly, we do. And don't think you'll be fooling either of us anymore. Your teachers are e-mailing the assignments to both of us, and we'll be checking on your work every night.

Jake: Great. Like prison.

Dad: Prison is where you're headed if you keep up this nonsense. Now get your work out and finish your homework. You will need to make up all missing work as well. This behavior ends. Now.

Jake: (He storms off, mumbling under his breath.)

The end of the conversation is a familiar one. The parents are angry. Jake is angry. I consider this a somewhat typical response in my work with parents, and one most of the parents would like to change.

New Dialogue Using Coaching Strategies

Difficult confrontations about behavioral missteps needn't end in the frustration evident throughout the preceding dialogue. Using empathy techniques and focusing on the relationships and social-emotional learning skills, parents can shift conversations into something more productive. Let's examine the new dialogue as one example of an empathy-oriented response:

Mom: Jake, your father and I spoke with your school this morning about your grades and your behaviors. Is there something you would like to tell us?

Jake: What do you mean?

The Caring Child

> *Mom:* Is there anything about your grades or your behaviors at school lately that we should discuss . . . anything you haven't told us that you would like to tell us now?

Mom is giving Jake opportunities to tell his parents the truth about school. She told him that she has already spoken with the school. By asking for him to speak, she is inviting him to share the information first. She is attempting to give him agency.

> *Jake:* Um . . . well . . . what did they tell you?
>
> *Dad:* They said you've been having some difficulties. What do you want to tell us about it?
>
> *Jake:* Did they say anything else?
>
> *Dad:* Jake, I imagine you must be a little afraid to tell us anything. I know I would feel that way if I was doing stuff my parents wouldn't like. It's okay to be scared. But I need you to be honest right now and tell us what's happening.

Jake is trying to get out of saying too much to his parents. He is protecting himself and trying to manipulate the situation. Rather than get caught up in his behavior, Jake's dad is using empathy to invite Jake to be honest. In this way, he is establishing a safe and caring space to have difficult conversations.

> *Jake:* Um . . . my grades have slipped a bit. And I sorta got into a fight with someone. It wasn't my fault though. He was bullying me, and I couldn't take it anymore.
>
> *Dad:* Anything else?
>
> *Jake:* I sorta wrote your name on the suspension form. I didn't want you guys to be mad. The guy had it coming, though. Seriously. He's been bullying me all year.

Empathy in the Home

Jake has shared some information. Although his parents' know that the information is incomplete and that Jake is shifting blame, they are continuing to be empathetic and trying to coach Jake:

Mom: It sounds like school has been really rough this semester. I'm sorry you didn't feel comfortable coming to us sooner, but I am glad we are talking now. Let's start with the classes. What are your current grades?

Jake: I know they aren't good. I've been too scared to check on them.

Mom: It's hard to admit when we are struggling, isn't it? Okay, can you check them now . . . on your phone?

Jake: Sure. (*Jake checks his grades.*)

By starting with the least emotional problem, Jake and his parents can gain the positive momentum they will need for the more difficult conversation to come. Here, Jake's mom uses empathy and focused questions to keep the conversation on track. From here, she can help Jake own the reality of his grades and strategize a solution. She can also ask why he feels it is difficult and make an action plan to make things better in the future.

Let's look at how she concludes the grade conversation and transitions to his behaviors:

Mom: How are you feeling about the plan to improve your grades?

Jake: Better. What if the work is too hard, though?

Mom: Well, what can you do if you start to struggle?

Jake: I can ask my teacher for help or you guys. Right?

Mom: Excellent. Yes, we are always here to help you. And if you need extra tutoring, we can do that. Jake, we all

---

need help from time to time. Better to ask for it early, than fail because you were too embarrassed. Okay?

Jake: Okay. Thanks, Mom.

Dad: Let's talk about the other situation now. The bullying. What's been happening?

Jake: A couple of guys are always picking on me—talking about you guys and saying I'm stupid. They never let up. I hate it.

Dad: That sounds rough. Have you told anyone about it?

Jake: What's the point? It's not like they're going to do anything about it. Everyone knows this happens, but nothing ever changes. One day I just had enough. I hit the guy.

Dad: It sounds like you were really angry.

Jake: I was.

Dad: And how did you feel after you hit the guy?

Jake: Honestly? Better. But only for a little while. Then I felt bad. And then scared. I knew I'd be in trouble. And I'm afraid the other guy is going to get me back.

Dad: So was violence the best solution now that you can look back on the choice?

Jake: No.

Dad: How about forging my signature? Was that the best choice?

Jake: No.

Dad: How do you think I feel about everything?

Jake: Like you can't trust me anymore. Like I really let you down.

Dad: That's correct. But guess what? I feel other things too— I'm sad that you are going through difficult times, sad that I wasn't there for you when everything happened or through the bullying that has been going on. You are very important to me. I want to be there for you when you are struggling. I want you to know that you can come to me. Understand?

Jake: Yeah, I think so.

Dad: So what should we do now? How can we rebuild the trust and move forward?

Jake and his parents can decide the consequences for his behavior at this point. No one will walk away angry. Using empathy responses and focusing on teaching the skills Jake was struggling with enabled a previously lose-lose conversation to turn into something more. Something better. See Tip Sheet 19: Coparenting Strategies for more tips.

TIP SHEET 19
Coparenting Strategies

» Be child-centered. Your children are the focus, not the issues between the two of you.

» Practice good communication skills.

» Assume positive intent. Not everything is about conflict.

» Communicate your needs and desires openly and honestly, but be prepared to compromise.

» Your children are the focus. Always. (And yes, I know this is stated twice—on purpose!)

The scenarios in this chapter were chosen to highlight the everyday opportunities you have as parents to constantly nurture the emotional intelligence of your children. It will feel strange, at first. You may not be used to engaging in empathy-oriented conversations with your children. Keep practicing. Short of abusive language, there are no wrong ways to talk with your children, per se—just ways that miss opportunities to deepen relationships and improve social-emotional functioning. As you take the action steps highlighted at the end of this chapter, be easy on yourself. Parenting is hard work. The responsibility is great. But so is the payoff. Take time to model empathy and compassion—for your children and yourself.

In the next chapter, the focus shifts from home to school. Just as many opportunities abound for this type of engagement at home, opportunities to nurture and develop emotional intelligence and resilience also exist at school.

Cultivating Caring Action Steps

Part III is all about taking action on the information presented throughout the book. Chapter 6 focused on real-world scenarios at home, showing both conversations with and without the strategies that build empathy and develop emotional intelligence. For your action steps, I want you to focus on the many ways you can incorporate empathy into daily life.

1. Keep a log of the daily conversations that involved, or could involve, empathy-oriented strategies.
2. Reflect on the conversations you logged, as well as any others you didn't decide to log. Were there opportunities to explore emotions, discuss feelings and behaviors, or model empathy that were not used? Why? Make a list of ways you could have incorporated more empathy into the conversations.
3. Commit to using empathy-related conversational strategies at home one time over the next week. What was the difference in the conversation? Once you are used to engaging in this type of discussion weekly, increase the number of conversations.

Empathy at School

Today's students struggle with both empathy and compassion. It is something I witness daily. And it is only getting worse. Anything we can do to help children develop these much-needed skills is not only welcomed, but desperately needed.
  —High school administrator and mother of a young child

SIMILAR to the many opportunities to build social-emotional skills available at home, school is an ideal place for students to learn and practice empathy, compassion, and emotional flexibility. Classroom activities, lunch and recess, and clubs all provide ample chances to practice and refine emotional intelligence skills through peer interactions, structured social-emotional lessons, collaborative groups, and conflict.

The following scenarios involve typical school behaviors, including noncompliance in the classroom, peer conflict, verbal aggression toward an adult, and returning to campus after a suspension. Within the role-plays are examples of the many opportunities to practice and develop empathy and compassion at school. In each situation, you

DOI: 10.4324/9781003238751-11

will get a picture of the missed opportunities for social-emotional coaching and ways to improve the various conversations.

Community Circles

One of the most impactful ways to build a positive school culture is through the use of community circles. Designed to build deeper adult-student and peer relationships, community circles are a widely used educational practice that involve sitting students in a circle and asking a variety of low-to-higher risk personal questions, discussing events of the day, and checking in with how students are feeling. Circles are also used as teaching strategies to foster caring environments in which academic risk-taking is the norm.

Community circles can occasionally be the center of conflict when students refuse to participate or violate the behavioral expectations for the circle. In the following scenario, a student's constant refusal to participate in the community circle leads to confrontation with the teacher and some of the students.

Scenario

José is a fifth-grade student in Ms. Walker's class. Every morning, the class starts with a community circle called "Morning Meeting" to check in, build relationships and class community, and set the tone for the day. Although students can choose not to talk in the circle, it is expected that all students will participate by sitting in the circle and following the behavioral expectations.

José struggles with Morning Meeting, often refusing to move his chair into a circle, talking out during the circle, and making fun of his peers. More than once, he has been asked to leave the circle due to his lack of behavior management.

In this scenario, José has disrupted the circle by mimicking a classmate with exceptional needs. Ms. Walker has asked him to return to his desk. José complied, but not without outbursts. He kicked a classmates chair on the way to his desk, pounded his fist on his desk, and mumbled profanity under his breath.

Initial Dialogue

Frustrated by the constant behavioral outbursts, Ms. Walker talks with José about his behavior.

Ms. Walker:	José, please come with me into the hallway.
José:	Why? What did I do?
Classmates:	*(The class jeers.)* Ooohh. You're in trouble. 'Bout time.
Ms. Walker:	Class, enough. Get to work on your journals. I will be back shortly. José?
José:	*(He gets up reluctantly and follows Ms. Walker into the hallway.)*
Ms. Walker:	José, I am very disappointed in your behavior. I've warned you several times to stop disrupting Morning Meeting, but nothing seems to work. You leave me no choice but to call your mother again and send you to the office.
José:	Whatever, I hate it here. Morning Meeting is stupid. This whole class is stupid.
Ms. Walker:	Is that what you really think?
José:	Yes.
Ms. Walker:	Fine. Then go to the office. I don't want you back in class until you can follow the rules and behave appropriately.
José:	I don't want to be here anyway.
Ms. Walker:	Get your backpack and go!
José:	*(He walks into class and grabs his backpack. On the way, he kicks the chair of a classmate.)* See you never!

| Ms. Walker: | (She tries to hand José an office referral form. He refuses to take the form and walks out of the class. Ms. Walker calls the office and reports that José has left the class without the referral form.) |

Analysis of Dialogue

In this scenario, Ms. Walker is understandably frustrated with José and sees no alternative but to refer him to school administration for disciplinary action. José is equally frustrated and not complying with adult instruction. He is lashing out at others and determined to refuse compliance. Although the teacher handled the situation in an appropriate manner, the opportunities for relationship building and empathy modeling were missed. This will likely result in further fracturing of social capital between José and Ms. Walker, and deepen the rift between them. It is doubtful that José will comply in the future based on the scenario, increasing the potential for more inappropriate behavior.

Let's examine the dialogue closely to see where a different approach from Ms. Walker could improve the outcomes for José and the class.

Ms. Walker:	José, please come with me into the hallway.
José:	Why? What did I do?
Classmates:	(The class jeers.) Ooohh. You're in trouble. 'Bout time.
Ms. Walker:	Class, enough. Get to work on your journals. I will be back shortly. José?
José:	(He gets up reluctantly and follows Ms. Walker into the hallway.)

On the surface, this looks like a typical conversation with no need for change. Ms. Walker is specific in her requests. What is lacking is the empathy needed to transform this from a purely corrective conversation to one that can both build the relationship between Ms. Walker and José and help him develop his social-emotional skills.

Ms. Walker: José, I am very disappointed in your behavior. I've warned you several times to stop disrupting Morning Meeting, but nothing seems to work. You leave me no choice but to call your mother again and send you to the office.

José: Whatever, I hate it here. Morning Meeting is stupid. This whole class is stupid.

Ms. Walker: Is that what you really think?

José: Yes.

Again, the lack of empathetic responses from Ms. Walker prevents this from being a transformative conversation. Opportunities for growth are missed, and the chances of changing the behavior over the long term are lost.

Ms. Walker: Fine. Then go to the office. I don't want you back in class until you can follow the rules and behave appropriately.

José: I don't want to be here anyway.

José is frustrated. Ms. Walker is frustrated. The conversation has deteriorated, and it is clear that nothing is going to be resolved.

Ms. Walker: Get your backpack and go!

José: (*He walks into class and grabs his backpack. On the way, he kicks the chair of a classmate.*) See you never!

| Ms. Walker: | (She tries to hand José an office referral form. He refuses to take the form and walks out of the class. Ms. Walker calls the office and reports that José has left the class without the referral form.) |

José is angry at this point, something made clear by his behavior. Ms. Walker is also angry. The scenario is predictable in its end and will result in further problems. There are no empathetic responses, no opportunities for José to look at his behavior and make new choices.

It would be easy to say that a teacher has no time to engage differently than Ms. Walker, that her response was the best anyone could do given the situation. However, it takes little time to change this into a more productive conversation. It is a matter of language choice and intent.

Take a look at the revised dialogue for an example of how one might respond differently and how that could change the probable outcome.

New Dialogue Using Coaching Strategies

In this new dialogue, Ms. Walker uses a more empathy-oriented response. Let's look at how the dynamic changes.

| Ms. Walker: | Class, please get out your journals and start working on the morning prompt on the board. (She walks to José's desk.) José, can you come with me to the hallway for just a moment. I want an opportunity to connect with you and check in. |

Immediately the tone of the conversation is different. Ms. Walker has given the class an assignment, taking their attention away from José. She has spoken to José individually and stated her intent as nonthreatening. This allows José to make the choice to go with her without needing to be defensive. It maintains communication without triggering inappropriate, trauma-based behaviors.

> *José:* Oh. Okay. *(José follows Ms. Walker into the hallway. He is surprised by the neutral request and less likely to be defensive.)*
>
> *Ms. Walker:* How are you this morning? I couldn't help but notice that it seems like you may be upset about something. Everything okay at home?

Ms. Walker is not focusing on José's poor behavior choices. Instead, she is attempting to get underneath the behavior and talk about why he was struggling. This empathetic approach enables her to try to get to the heart of the problem quickly and communicates caring.

> *José:* I'm okay, I guess. I just hate the Morning Meeting. It's stupid.
>
> *Ms. Walker:* I'm sorry that you feel that way. Do you understand why I think it is important that we do them?
>
> *José:* You want to get to know us more. But what if I don't want anyone to know more about me?
>
> *Ms. Walker:* That's right. I do want to know my students well. I want all of us to know each other so that we can better understand each other. It's okay if you are not comfortable sharing. You are allowed to stay silent in the circle.

Ms. Walker and José are having a meaningful conversation about the task that José has disrupted. She is explaining her perspective and respecting his. This enables José to practice his social-emotional skills and voice his concerns and needs.

José:	Other kids bug me if I do.
Ms. Walker:	That's not okay. How does it make you feel when they do that?
José:	Angry. Like I want to hit them.
Ms. Walker:	It must be hard to feel that way every time we have Morning Meeting. Is that why you act out?
José:	Maybe. I guess so.
Ms. Walker:	That makes sense to me. But when you act out it makes it very hard for me to conduct the meeting. It takes away from what the circle time is trying to accomplish. And it makes me sad. I'm not able to get to know you, and my ability to help the class is reduced. Do you understand?
José:	Yeah. I think so.

In this exchange, both parties are able to express their feelings in a healthy way. It models an empathy-oriented conversation and paves the way for more conversations in the future.

Let's see how the conversation ends.

Ms. Walker:	I'd like us to try again. You don't have to talk in the circles. We will go over the meeting rules with everyone so that the other kids don't pressure you or anyone else to talk. Do you think we can try again?
José:	Okay.
Ms. Walker:	What should we do about your behavior today? How can we make things right?
José:	(He thinks for a moment.) I guess I could apologize. Maybe stay in at recess and clean the classroom or something?
Ms. Walker:	Those are very good ideas. Let's pick one of those things to do.

In this version of the conversation, the student is not sent out of the classroom. He is no longer triggered by the teacher or other students and manages to stay in control of his behavior. The behavior expectations are made clearer, a game plan for the future is developed, and a consequence for the behavior is established. This conversation would not take more time, and the results are significantly more positive for the student, the teacher, and the classroom environment. See Tip Sheet 20: Strategies for Successful Circles for more information.

TIP SHEET 20
Strategies for Successful Circles

Classroom circles are a popular way to build trust and community in the classroom environment. Conducting successful circles involves creating a caring culture and developing positive relationships. The following tips can help you as you establish the practice of classroom circles in your classroom:

» **Start With Norms and Expectations:** It is important to establish expectations for circle behaviors at the start of the practice. Have students help establish the expectations and hold each other accountable. Teach and review the expectations frequently.

» **Acknowledge and Correct Behaviors Quickly:** Don't let bad habits take hold. Acknowledge both appropriate and inappropriate behavior as it happens, with a plan for correcting any behavioral missteps.

» **Focus on Low-Risk Questions First:** Circles are powerful tools for getting to deep, emotional topics. But it requires trust and safety for students to "go there"—and that takes time to develop. Start with easy questions like "What is your favorite color?" or "What are you looking forward to this weekend?" before jumping into the deep stuff.

TIP SHEET 20, *continued*

> » **Participate Alongside Your Students:** The purpose of circles is to build community. Answer the questions along with your students. Don't be afraid for them to see you as a person first and their teacher second.

Peer Relationships

Peer relationships are a natural way for students to grow and develop social-emotional learning skills, including empathy and compassion. Through opportunities for group collaboration and even conflict, students get a chance to see the world through another's eyes.

In the following scenario, two girls in middle school have a conflict and are sent to the counseling office.

Scenario

Naomi and Jasmine are seventh-grade girls attending the same middle school. Friends for the past 5 years, the girls are struggling with each other. Jasmine has a new set of friends and doesn't want to hang out with Naomi anymore. Naomi doesn't understand why things are different.

Initial Dialogue

In an attempt to talk things out, Naomi approached Jasmine at lunch to talk. She yelled and Naomi and insulted her, resulting in a verbal altercation at the lunch tables. Both girls were sent to the counseling office to speak with Ms. Anderson, a counseling intern.

Empathy at School

Ms. Anderson: Hello, Naomi and Jasmine. I understand you are having some difficulties getting along. Can you tell me what happened?

Jasmine: *(Starts talking over Naomi)* I told Naomi I didn't want to hang out anymore. She won't leave me alone now. She's like a total stalker. When she came up to me at lunch, I lost it and told her to leave me alone. I have a right to make new friends without her hounding me.

Naomi: *(She looks down at the floor.)*

Ms. Anderson: Naomi? Do you have anything to add?

Naomi: *(She shakes her head "no.")*

Ms. Anderson: Okay. Well, you are correct, Jasmine, that you can make new friends. But at this school we try to get along with everyone. Although you do have a right to eat your lunch in peace, yelling at Naomi wasn't the best way to handle your frustration.

Jasmine: Well, she needs to respect my space.

Naomi: I didn't get in your space. I asked you a question.

Jasmine: After I already told you to leave me alone. You are so needy all of the time. This is why I can't be your friend anymore. You're suffocating.

Naomi: Sorry I care.

Jasmine: Whatever. I don't think you care about me. You just don't like being alone. No one wants to be around your needy self.

Naomi: *(She stares at the floor again.)*

Jasmine: Nothing left to say? Didn't think so. Ms. Anderson, can I go now?

Ms. Anderson: Not just yet. Naomi, can you apologize to Jasmine for not respecting her request to be left alone? And

> Jasmine, can you apologize to Naomi for yelling at her during lunch?

Jasmine: As long as she stays away from me, sure. Sorry I yelled at you because you won't stop bugging me.

Ms. Anderson: Thank you. Naomi?

Naomi: *(Mumbles softly)* Sorry.

Ms. Anderson: A little louder please.

Naomi: Sorry.

Ms. Anderson: You girls can leave now. I expect that this is the end of the problem, okay?

Jasmine: Yep.

Naomi: *(She nods.)*

Analysis of Dialogue

In this scenario, both girls have broken trust with each other and used embarrassing truths to cause emotional or social pain. It was a perfect opportunity to talk about the problem openly to help both girls see from the others' perspectives.

Let's examine the dialogue closely to see where a different response could have changed the conversation completely:

Ms. Anderson: Hello, Naomi and Jasmine. I understand you are having some difficulties getting along. Can you tell me what happened?

Jasmine: *(Starts talking over Naomi)* I told Naomi I didn't want to hang out anymore. She won't leave me alone now. She's like a total stalker. When she came up to me at lunch, I lost it and told her to leave me alone. I have a right to make new friends without her hounding me.

Naomi:	*(She looks down at the floor.)*
Ms. Anderson:	Naomi? Do you have anything to add?
Naomi:	*(She shakes her head "no.")*
Ms. Anderson:	Okay. Well, you are correct, Jasmine, that you can make new friends. But at this school we try to get along with everyone. Although you do have a right to eat your lunch in peace, yelling at Naomi wasn't the best way to handle your frustration.

It's clear that Naomi is uncomfortable in the setting with Jasmine. This immediately creates communication roadblocks. Jasmine's tone and language contribute to the unbalanced nature of the conversation. This could predictably end in increased conflict and the potential for additional harm to at least one of the participants.

Jasmine:	Well, she needs to respect my space.
Naomi:	I didn't get in your space. I asked you a question.
Jasmine:	After I already told you to leave me alone. You are so needy all of the time. This is why I can't be your friend anymore. You're suffocating.
Naomi:	Sorry I care.
Jasmine:	Whatever. I don't think you care about me. You just don't like being alone. No one wants to be around your needy self.
Naomi:	*(She stares at the floor again.)*

The conversation is dominated by Jasmine with no interjection from Ms. Anderson. This increases the social imbalance and contributes to Naomi's increased detachment from the conversation. No appropriate resolutions are possible at this point.

Jasmine:	Nothing left to say? Didn't think so. Ms. Anderson, can I go now?
Ms. Anderson:	Not just yet. Naomi, can you apologize to Jasmine for not respecting her request to be left alone? And Jasmine, can you apologize to Naomi for yelling at her during lunch?
Jasmine:	As long as she stays away from me, sure. Sorry I yelled at you because you won't stop bugging me.

It's clear that no actual resolution is occurring. The apology from Jasmine is not rooted in any perspective or empathy. It is reasonable to assume the behavior of both girls will continue.

Ms. Anderson:	Thank you. Naomi?
Naomi:	*(Mumbles softly)* Sorry.
Ms. Anderson:	A little louder please.
Naomi:	Sorry.
Ms. Anderson:	You girls can leave now. I expect that this is the end of the problem, okay?
Jasmine:	Yep.
Naomi:	*(She nods.)*

Throughout the scenario, it is clear that Ms. Anderson is not focused on restoring the relationship between the girls, growing empathy, or helping the girls increase social-emotional skills. With a different, empathy-oriented response, it is possible to cultivate an opportunity for growth, regardless of the changing relationship status between the participants.

Empathy at School

New Dialogue Using Coaching Strategies

Peer conflicts can be tricky to navigate. Approaching the conversation with empathy and compassion can defuse much of the emotion. Using many of the strategies discussed throughout the book can help. Let's see how the dialogue and outcome change as a result of subtle shifts in language and intent.

Ms. Anderson:	Hello, Naomi and Jasmine. I'd like to talk with you about the incident at lunch. But before we start, let's establish a few ground rules—norms, I like to call them. First, this is a safe space. What we talk about here needs to stay here. The only exceptions are if you say something about hurting yourself, hurting others, or if someone is hurting you. Do you understand? *(Jasmine and Naomi nod in unison.)*
Ms. Anderson:	Next, we speak with respect and not insults. We respect each other's point of view and don't speak over or interrupt each other. Finally, we are honest and speak about what we think and feel, not what we assume the other person thinks and feels. Sound good?
Jasmine:	Cool.
Naomi:	Okay. *(Naomi whispers.)*
Ms. Anderson:	Do either of you want to add anything to the norms? *(Both girls are silent.)*
Ms. Anderson:	Okay. Let's start with you, Naomi. What happened at lunch? How did things start?

Ms. Anderson leads the conversation from the beginning, establishing safety and social balance. She sets expectations and conveys a positive intent. After recognizing Naomi as the more socially reserved participant (through recognition of social cues), she invites Naomi to start with her perspective.

Naomi: I went up to Jasmine to ask her a question. She got angry and yelled at me. So I yelled back.

Jasmine: That's not exactly how things happened.

Ms. Anderson: Hold on, Jasmine. I have some clarifying questions first. Then I want to hear your perspective. Okay?

Jasmine: Fine.

Ms. Anderson is maintaining authority in the conversation while respecting both girls. She conveys respect to both participants through her responses to the girls.

Ms. Anderson: You and Jasmine used to be close friends, yes? I imagine her response upset you.

Naomi: Yes. I was trying to talk to her to find out why we weren't friends anymore. I just want to be her friend. But when she yelled I got mad, too.

Ms. Anderson: (*Ms. Anderson signals Jasmine, who is about to speak, to wait.*) Yes, I can understand being mad. I am wondering, though, if Jasmine interpreted you coming up to her at lunch differently. Let's hear your side, Jasmine. Okay?

Jasmine: I told Naomi that I wanted nothing to do with her or our past friendship. But she can't take "no" for an answer. She's so needy.

Ms. Anderson: Tell me what you feel, not Naomi's feelings or thoughts. What were you thinking or feeling when she approached you about the friendship again?

Using reflection and empathy, Ms. Anderson is able to keep Jasmine focused on her thoughts and feelings. Let's see how she guides the conversation to a solution.

Jasmine:	I was angry. I still am. I don't understand why she can't just go and find new friends. I want her to leave me alone.
Ms. Anderson:	I can hear your anger. I'm sure it is frustrating to not feel heard in this situation.
Jasmine:	It really is!
Ms. Anderson:	Is it possible that Naomi has been feeling unheard as well?
Jasmine:	Maybe, I guess. But, I don't see how.
Ms. Anderson:	Let's find out. Naomi, how have you felt since Jasmine told you she wanted to end the friendship?
Naomi:	Really hurt. I keep asking why, and all she says is to leave her alone. What did I do, Jasmine?
Ms. Anderson:	You know, it's not unusual for friendships to change, even end, for no clear reason. What I want you both to recognize is that you feel similar things. Jasmine, you are feeling disrespected and unheard. This has made you angry. Naomi, you are also feeling disrespected and unheard. You are hurt and angry. Is this pretty accurate? Did I capture your words correctly? *(Both girls nod in agreement.)*
Ms. Anderson:	Is there anything else you want the other person to know?
Naomi:	*(She shakes her head "no.")*
Jasmine:	I guess not. Well, I really want to be left alone—at least for now.
Ms. Anderson:	Naomi, do you understand where Jasmine is coming from . . . what she is asking?
Naomi:	*(She nods.)*
Ms. Anderson:	Can you respect it for now?
Naomi:	Yes. It's just hard. I miss you, Jasmine.

The Caring Child

Jasmine: Thanks. I just need some space. Okay?

Naomi: *(She nods again.)*

Ms. Anderson: Are you girls willing to move forward?

Jasmine: Sure.

Naomi: Yes.

Ms. Anderson: And what will you do at lunch tomorrow?

Naomi: I'll leave Jasmine alone and sit somewhere else.

Jasmine: Thank you. That's all I was trying to ask.

Naomi: I'm sorry I wasn't respectful.

Jasmine: I'm sorry I yelled at you in front of the whole school.

Ms. Anderson: I think we've made some progress here. I would like to speak with you both in the future, okay. Just to check in individually with you. Would that be alright?

In this scenario, Ms. Anderson helps the girls begin to understand each other's feelings. No one is wronged for her individual feelings or thoughts. There is no attempt to force a relationship. Boundaries are allowed and encouraged. Although Naomi is not getting what she wants, she is able to begin to learn that social connections change. Sometimes the change feels good. Sometimes it hurts. Learning to ebb and flow through relationships is important.

For Jasmine, she was given an opportunity to see that she and Naomi were feeling similar emotions. This is important and builds both empathy and compassion. See Tip Sheet 21: Toxic Relationship Busters to utilize yourself or share with students or children.

TIP SHEET 21
Toxic Relationship Busters

Not all relationships are healthy. Sometimes, friendships diminish your self-esteem and resiliency. These are toxic and need to change. The following tips help you recognize when a relationship is no longer working and do something about it:

» **Pay Attention to How You Feel in the Relationship:** If you experience high levels of emotional distress or discomfort in your relationship, that is a sure sign that something is wrong. Check in with yourself often and take action if your distress continues.

» **Focus on Yourself First:** Relationships are partnerships. To make them effective and mutually beneficial it is important for each person to know what his or her needs are and communicate them to each other. Taking time to build your personal resilience and understand what you need from a relationship is a critical step in forming healthy bonds.

» **Practice Healthy Boundaries:** For a relationship to work, everyone needs to practice healthy boundaries. This applies to emotional and physical boundaries. Establish and maintain them early in the relationship. If your friend or partner violates them, be sure to address it. If you find yourself growing enmeshed in the other due to weak emotional boundaries, take a moment to put yourself in check. No one benefits from unhealthy boundaries.

» **Be Willing to Leave:** Staying in an unhealthy relationship benefits no one. Be willing to leave the friendship if things are toxic. If you can't eliminate contact (due to school or work), be willing to distance yourself and reestablish strong boundaries.

Verbal Aggression

One of the most troubling behaviors in schools is verbal aggression. Students who make threats, use profanity directed at others, or engage in bullying behavior disrupt the learning environment for both students and staff. Although this behavior is often subject to significant disciplinary actions, suspension and other exclusionary practices have not been shown to change the students' inappropriate behavior. In fact, many times, students return from disciplinary action less connected to school and less willing to be part of the educational community (Center for Promise, 2018). Pairing an empathy-focused strategy with the required disciplinary action has a greater likelihood of resulting in long-term change for the student and improving the school climate.

The following scenario takes a look at the conversation between a student and the dean of discipline at a high school following a verbal altercation with a teacher. See the difference an empathy-oriented approach can make to the long-term outcome for the student and the school.

Scenario

Henry is a tenth-grade student in a comprehensive high school. He has struggled with his behavior throughout his educational career, often engaging in verbal disputes with both his peers and his teachers. One day, Henry's behaviors escalate in class. His math teacher, Mr. Johnson, asks him to start an assignment. Henry refuses and proceeds to bother the students next to him. His teacher again asks him to start his work. Henry refuses. On the third attempt, Mr. Johnson explains that he will have to ask Henry to go to the dean's office if he doesn't settle in and start his work. Henry yells "F&$^ you!" to his teacher, throws his book on the ground, and leaves the class. Mr. Johnson calls the office and alerts campus security to the situation. Henry is found and escorted to the dean's office.

132

Empathy at School

Initial Dialogue

In this scenario, Mr. Alvarado, the dean of discipline, talks with Henry about the incident.

Mr. Alvarado: Henry, why weren't you in class?

Henry: I was just going to the bathroom.

Mr. Alvarado: Let's agree not to lie to each other, shall we? I will ask again, why did you leave your math class?

Henry: I'm not lying. I had to go to the bathroom.

Mr. Alvarado: Did you leave with permission?

Henry: (He stays silent.)

Mr. Alvarado: Henry?

Henry: I don't know what the big deal is. I just went to the bathroom.

Mr. Alvarado: Both Mr. Johnson and Ms. Gomez said you were out of class without permission. Furthermore, Mr. Johnson said you used profanity before leaving. This is your opportunity to tell me what happened. Otherwise, I will have no choice but to act on the information I have right now.

Henry: This is so lame. You are just going to believe everything Mr. Johnson and Ms. Gomez say anyway. Why don't you just suspend me and let me go already?

Mr. Alvarado: Should I suspend you?

Henry: Whatever! I don't care. Do whatever you want. This school is so lame.

Mr. Alvarado: Fine. You are suspended for the rest of the day and tomorrow. Take a seat in the office while I call your mom.

Henry: (He gets up and shoves a chair as he leaves the office.)

Mr. Alvarado: None of that, Henry, or things will get worse.

     Henry: (He ignores Mr. Alvarado as he mumbles under his breath.)

Analysis of Dialogue

In this scenario, the student, Henry, has clearly violated school rules and could certainly be suspended for his behavior. The dean's interactions with the student are normal and not indicative of specific concerns. But, similar to the other role-plays, Mr. Alvarado has missed opportunities to help Henry see the impact of his behavioral choices, own that impact, and grow social-emotional skills. Furthermore, the opportunities to repair harm caused to the classroom community and the relationship between Henry and Mr. Johnson, the teacher, were lost in this dialogue. It is doubtful that Henry will return from the suspension having learned how to make new behavioral choices or increase his social capital with Mr. Johnson.

Let's examine the dialogue closely to see where opportunities for improved student outcomes were lost.

Mr. Alvarado: Henry, why weren't you in class?

     Henry: I was just going to the bathroom.

Mr. Alvarado: Let's agree not to lie to each other, shall we? I will ask again, why did you leave your math class?

Although Mr. Alvarado has information that verifies Henry's initial lie, calling him out on it automatically shifts the conversation into a full-blown confrontation.

     Henry: I'm not lying. I had to go to the bathroom.

Mr. Alvarado: Did you leave with permission?

Henry: (He stays silent.)

Mr. Alvarado: Henry?

Henry: I don't know what the big deal is. I just went to the bathroom.

Mr. Alvarado is trying to move Henry to admit his wrongdoings. However, because the conversation had already shifted toward a confrontation, Henry has no trust that he will be heard. Without that trust, he is unwilling to risk owning his behavior or even participating in the conversation in a meaningful way.

Mr. Alvarado: Both Mr. Johnson and Ms. Gomez said you were out of class without permission. Furthermore, Mr. Johnson said you used profanity before leaving. This is your opportunity to tell me what happened. Otherwise, I will have no choice but to act on the information I have right now.

Henry: This is so lame. You are just going to believe everything Mr. Johnson and Ms. Gomez say anyway. Why don't you just suspend me and let me go already?

Mr. Alvarado: Should I suspend you?

Henry: Whatever! I don't care. Do whatever you want. This school is so lame.

By now, both parties' emotions are escalating. Although Mr. Alvarado is doing a good job trying to allow multiple opportunities for Henry to engage appropriately and take ownership for the behavior, too much is lost already. A different initial engagement, or a purposeful switch of conversation focus, is necessary to provide the trust and safety needed for Henry to respond in a different way.

Mr. Alvarado: Fine. You are suspended for the rest of the day and tomorrow. Take a seat in the office while I call your mom.

Henry: (He gets up and shoves a chair as he leaves the office.)

Mr. Alvarado: None of that, Henry, or things will get worse.

Henry: (He ignores Mr. Alvarado as he mumbles under his breath.)

At this point, the conversation is over, and both Henry and Mr. Alvarado are frustrated. Henry did not own his behavior or learn ways to improve in the future. Mr. Alvarado was not able to do anything other than follow through with the previously defined consequence. Both parties remain unheard and frustrated. No repairs to relationships or school engagement have been accomplished.

New Dialogue Using Coaching Strategies

In this new dialogue, see how empathy-oriented and restorative conversations pave the way for improved outcomes for the student and the classroom.

Mr. Alvarado: Hello, Henry. How are you today?

Henry: (He shrugs and looks down.)

Mr. Alvarado: Mr. Johnson tells me that math was a struggle today. I'd like to know what happened? Were there some difficulties in class? Maybe with the work or something?

In this dialogue, Mr. Alvarado isn't focusing on the behavioral concern initially. Instead, he is demonstrating positive intent and concern by reframing the behavior in neutral terms and allowing the student to express the difficulty.

Henry: (Henry looks up suspiciously.) What else did he say?

Empathy at School

Mr. Alvarado:	He was concerned. He said you appeared angry and said some things you normally don't say to him.
Henry:	(He stays silent.)
Mr. Alvarado:	What's up, Henry? Is math giving you problems?
Henry:	It's not that exactly. I just had a bad morning.
Mr. Alvarado:	Is it anything you want to talk about?

Mr. Alvarado is working to establish trust and reaffirming the positive intent and concern.

Henry:	Not really.
Mr. Alvarado:	Okay. And what happened in class?
Henry:	Mr. Johnson kept bugging me to get to work. But I couldn't.
Mr. Alvarado:	You couldn't what . . . focus . . . do the work? I'm not sure I understand.
Henry:	I couldn't focus.
Mr. Alvarado:	You said you had a hard morning. Is that why it was hard to focus in class?
Henry:	Yeah.
Mr. Alvarado:	And Mr. Johnson was trying to get you to focus and do your work?
Henry:	Yeah. I didn't mean to get mad. He just wouldn't let up.
Mr. Alvarado:	Did you say or do something when you were angry?
Henry:	I just wanted him to back off. I couldn't stand being in there.
Mr. Alvarado:	Sounds like you were very upset.
Henry:	Yeah.

The Caring Child

As the conversation continues, Mr. Alvarado continues to ask questions and reflect back Henry's answers. This is done to ensure accurate communication and give Henry a voice. The segment ends with empathetic reflection of potential feelings. The goal is to maintain a safe and caring environment in which Henry can reflect on his behavior and own both his emotions and behavioral choices.

Mr. Alvarado: What do you think Mr. Johnson felt after you left?

Henry: Mad, I guess. I don't know. He called security to get me.

Mr. Alvarado: He had to do that. Do you know why?

Henry: I'm not supposed to leave class without permission.

Mr. Alvarado: It's more than that, you know. He is responsible for you, for your safety. He wanted to make sure you were okay.

Henry: (He looks down.)

Mr. Alvarado: How are you feeling now . . . still angry with Mr. Johnson . . . still upset about the morning at home?

Using empathy-oriented conversational techniques, Mr. Alvarado is attempting to help Henry see Mr. Johnson's perspective, develop empathy, and continue the conversation. Opportunities are provided to move forward and resolve the situation, but only after ensuring that Henry is ready to move forward and begin to take ownership for his behavior.

Henry: I guess I'm okay. I didn't mean to get mad.

Mr. Alvarado: I know you didn't. However, what are the school rules about using profanity with a staff member?

Henry: Are you going to suspend me?

Mr. Alvarado: Should I suspend you?

Henry: My dad will get mad.

Empathy at School

Mr. Alvarado:	I can understand that. I'd be angry if my child was suspended, too. What do you think would be an appropriate response for your behavior?
Henry:	Me? I don't know.
Mr. Alvarado:	Well, let's figure it out. You did break the rule, yes?
Henry:	I did.
Mr. Alvarado:	And we normally suspend for that, right?
Henry:	I guess.
Mr. Alvarado:	So should we suspend?
Henry:	(*He is quiet for a while before responding.*) Maybe I apologize to Mr. Johnson and ask to try again.
Mr. Alvarado:	Do you think that is enough? What happens the next time you are mad?
Henry:	Is there something I could learn to help me with that—being mad?
Mr. Alvarado:	There is. Should we try that?
Henry:	Yeah.
Mr. Alvarado:	And your parents? This is a serious offense. What should we do about that?

Throughout this part of the conversation, Mr. Alvarado coaches Henry to be able to accept some responsibility for his behavior and determine a way to make amends. Henry has a consequence for his behavior. He also has some agency in what that consequence is and how he can learn and move forward. This is the crux of a restorative and empathy-oriented conversation. The goals are to help children grow their social-emotional skills, demonstrate empathy, and deepen relationships with caring adults.

At this point, Mr. Alvarado and Henry can figure out the best solutions to all concerned parties. This type of conversation may take longer. It requires more effort and focus. But the results are profound and can result in long-term, positive change for the student.

Suspension Aftermath

Despite every attempt to create positive school environments and a restorative process for responding to behavioral concerns, suspensions can and do occur. When students return from suspension, however, there are seldom more than a few words spoken with an administrator before the student reengages with the school community. This is a major missed opportunity to check in with the student's feelings, repair any harm to the relationship between the student and the school, reset behavior expectations, and provide additional opportunities to learn and practice social-emotional skills.

Using the empathy-oriented techniques modeled in this section and discussed throughout the book, administration and counseling teams can welcome students back from a suspension with compassion. Arranging a meeting between the student, parents, and a school-based team is an important step in re-engaging the student back into the school environment. During this meeting, the school team can repair any harm caused by the behavior and corresponding suspension, remind the student of the expectations, and arrange for further social-emotional skill learning and practice opportunities. In this way, the suspension does not have to further create a rift between the student and the school. All parties can move forward and embrace the situation as an opportunity to learn and strengthen empathy, resilience, and emotional intelligence.

Cultivating Caring Action Steps

This chapter's scenarios focused on typical behavioral missteps within the educational setting. Teachers, school staff, and parents have opportunities to support and nurture the whole student. This happens when every opportunity to develop positive relationships and cultivate a caring climate is used. It is easy to forget about the impact teachers can have on students. Teachers commonly focus on the content of their teaching first, missing opportunities to increase social capital and enhance learning through emotional intelligence. It may seem that taking the time to engage in deeper conversations is not part of the job.

Actually, it is everyone's job. The adage "it takes a village" has never been truer. Students need parents *and* teachers to model caring, empathy, and compassion. Students need support from the many aspects of their lives in order to combat the negative outcomes possible in our digital age.

As a parent or teacher, take the time to reflect on your conversations with children. Teachers can consider the following questions, and parents can share them with teachers: Have you seized every moment to nurture positive relationships? Are you more focused on the content of your teaching than the environment the teaching occurs in? Do you believe that building social-emotional learning skills will enhance learning? Your answers to these questions will help you navigate the many competing activities that fill the school day. Focus on the needs of students—they are counting on you.

As we come to the last chapter, the focus shifts once again back to the home environment and the larger world. Our children are faced with big events throughout their lives. Chapter 8 examines a few of those events and ways to talk with children about the "big" stuff.

For these action steps, I want you to focus on the many ways you can incorporate opportunities to model, learn, and practice social-emotional development into every conversation with children. Keep track of the conversations you are currently having, and look for ways to infuse more empathy and compassion.

1. Reflect on the current school year. Have you engaged in meaningful conversations about emotions, empathy, and compassion with your children (or with your students)? If yes, what can you do to go even deeper? If no, what are the

barriers to this type of dialogue, and what can you do to move through these obstacles?

2. Reflect on the current classroom practices in your child's classroom (or your classroom). Is there a focus on the components necessary to create a caring classroom—including nurturing positive relationships, defining expectations, explicitly teaching social-emotional skills, and cultivating safety through common classroom routines and predictable adult responses to behavioral missteps? Make a plan for each component you'd like to target for improvement either at home or at school.

3. Commit to using empathy-oriented conversation strategies with your child (or at least one student) over the next month.

8

Empathy in the World

I feel like the world has gotten angry. Mean. It would be easy to say this is related to my generation, but I think that is the easy answer. We've forgotten how to communicate with each other. And while I do believe my generation is more tolerant than my parents', we don't know what to do with that tolerance other than voice our concerns as loudly as we can. We don't know how to take action and change the system, no matter how much we want to. Honestly, it feels very overwhelming at times.

—High school junior

CHAPTERS 6 and 7 focused on the many opportunities to grow empathy and compassion within the home and school settings. Now it is time to focus on the greater community and worldview. News stories about violence, injustice, and death can overwhelm children and adults alike. So much so that many families have opted to ignore the news entirely. Although balance is certainly important, and there is no reason to immerse yourself in the negative culture of a 24-hour news cycle, it is important to recognize what is happening in the world and seize the opportunities to practice and model emotional

143

DOI: 10.4324/9781003238751-12

flexibility wherever you can find them. Our children are exposed to world events, no matter how much we may want to shelter our kids from them.

I remember when my oldest child was about 8 years old. I was making dinner in the kitchen, and I had the news playing in the background, a familiar thing in my home. My daughter walked in just as the newscaster spoke about an 8-year-old girl who had been abducted and murdered. Before I could mute the sound or react in some other way, my daughter fixated on the news. She stood stone-still, listening to the newscaster's words. A picture flashed of the young girl. She looked similar to my daughter, and I knew my daughter was experiencing something new—a loss of innocence as she understood, maybe for the first time, that the world can be a mean place. She understood murder and death. And perhaps she was beginning to understand her own mortality.

I stopped making dinner in that moment and took the time to answer her many questions and talk about the news story. Would it have been easier to ignore what was happening, change the channel, and just make dinner? Absolutely. But as uncomfortable as that moment was, it was the perfect opportunity to talk about the world and safety. It was a chance to explore empathy and compassion, answer her questions and reestablish her safety, and allow her to grieve for this girl who felt so familiar.

The following scenarios involve some of the larger events that can impact our children and provide opportunities for deep conversations, even when such opportunities are uncomfortable or unwanted. Like the role-plays in the previous chapters, each scene provides an example of both the missed opportunities and how to intentionally create the space for deeper learning and the practice of social-emotional skills.

Violence in the News

It's hard to turn on the news and not hear about incredible acts of violence happening within the community and around the world. School shootings, acts of terrorism, and random acts of violence down the street—sooner or later, opportunities to talk about the violence that surrounds us will occur. Most of the time, we allow those moments to pass, not wanting to scare our children or break their foundation of safety and security. I understand that reaction. And, in some cases, talking about violence causes far more harm than the potential benefit. When children are living with high levels of complex trauma or dealing with multiple adverse experiences, the violence present in their everyday lives is more than they can handle. In these cases, other approaches to manage and move through the impact of trauma (like those found in my forthcoming book *Healing the Heart: Helping Your Child Thrive After Trauma*; Fonseca, 2020) may be most appropriate. For most of us, however, talking about the realities of the violence that exists in our world affords very specific opportunities to strengthen empathy and compassion.

In the following scenario, a child has heard about a school shooting from a friend and has many questions for her parents.

Scenario

Laney is a 10-year-old girl attending her neighborhood elementary school. Last week, a school shooting happened at a school in a neighboring town. Although Laney's parents don't watch the news very often or discuss events like the shooting in their home, Laney heard about the shooting from her classmates and teachers. The event left her scared to attend school for fear of something similar happening at her school. She told her teacher and the school nurse about her concerns. They told her that she was safe and suggested she talk with her parents. Laney decided that was exactly what she was going to do.

The Caring Child

Initial Dialogue

When Laney came home from school, she immediately asked about the school shooting, telling her mother about her concerns.

Mom: Hi, sweetie. How was school today?

Laney: I don't like school anymore. I don't think I want to go back.

Mom: You loved school this morning. What happened?

Laney: I heard my friends and some of the teachers talking about a school shooting. It scared me. I don't think I should go to school anymore.

Mom: I see. What did you hear?

Laney: Well, my friends said their parents wanted to keep them home. That no school is really safe anymore.

Mom: What did the teachers say?

Laney: I heard two of them talking in the library, and they said that teachers should be armed now. But I don't want to go to school in a place where everyone has guns. That doesn't seem safe to me. I asked my teacher about it. And the nurse.

Mom: You did? What did they say?

Laney: That schools are safe and I don't need to worry about anything. But I don't think that is right either. I Googled it on the way home, and there are a lot of school shootings. Schools aren't safe at all. So, I think I should stay home with you. You can teach me.

Mom: You are right. The world is a scary place right now. But I want you to go to school still. I wouldn't be a good teacher. And besides, you'd miss your friends.

Laney: But what if something happens?

> *Mom:* Nothing will happen, Laney. Not here. Your school is really safe. And your teachers have all been trained for emergencies. You have nothing to worry about. Now tell me about your homework.
>
> *Laney:* But—
>
> *Mom:* Laney, you're safe. I don't want you to stress over this. I just want you to be a kid. Now, what about your homework?

Analysis of Dialogue

In this scenario, Laney is struggling to feel safe after hearing about a school shooting from her friends and teachers. The ensuing conversation with her mother has a lot of strong points. However, there are numerous missed opportunities to deepen empathy and combat anxiety with action. Take a look at some of the missed opportunities as I analyze the conversation.

> *Mom:* Hi, sweetie. How was school today?
>
> *Laney:* I don't like school anymore. I don't think I want to go back.
>
> *Mom:* You loved school this morning. What happened?
>
> *Laney:* I heard my friends and some of the teachers talking about a school shooting. It scared me. I don't think I should go to school anymore.
>
> *Mom:* I see. What did you hear?
>
> *Laney:* Well, my friends said their parents wanted to keep them home. That no school is really safe anymore.

The Caring Child

Laney's mother does a nice job asking clarifying questions. However, she misses opportunities to reflect and model empathy. This is the most common omission I see when working with families. Although there is no specific harm caused by this, there is no intentional empathy growth or practice either.

Mom: What did the teachers say?

Laney: I heard two of them talking in the library, and they said that teachers should be armed now. But I don't want to go to school in a place where everyone has guns. That doesn't seem safe to me. I asked my teacher about it. And the nurse.

Mom: You did? What did they say?

Again, Laney's mom does a good job asking clarifying questions. But there are some spots here for validation and empathy that are missed.

Laney: That schools are safe and I don't need to worry about anything. But I don't think that is right either. I Googled it on the way home, and there are a lot of school shootings. Schools aren't safe at all. So, I think I should stay home with you. You can teach me.

Mom: You are right. The world is a scary place right now. But I want you to go to school still. I wouldn't be a good teacher. And besides, you'd miss your friends.

Although Laney's mom does do some validating in this section, rather than talk through the big emotions her daughter is feeling and maybe even discuss her fear, there is a shift away from emotions altogether. This effectively shuts down the potential for further conversations.

> *Laney:* But what if something happens?
>
> *Mom:* Nothing will happen, Laney. Not here. Your school is really safe. And your teachers have all been trained for emergencies. You have nothing to worry about. Now tell me about your homework.

Mom's fear and need to end the conversation have taken over. Although it is important to reassure your children about safety, Mom's inability to talk about the scenario has made it impossible to model empathy or compassion, let alone enact potential strategies to alleviate Laney's fears.

> *Laney:* But—
>
> *Mom:* Laney, you're safe. I don't want you to stress over this. I just want you to be a kid. Now, what about your homework?

At this point, the conversation is over. It is doubtful that Laney's concerns have been addressed. Shifting the conversation away from the issue only sends the message that this is not the type of thing Laney should discuss with her mom.

New Dialogue Using Coaching Strategies

This scenario shows how easy it is to miss key opportunities to build social-emotional skills throughout our daily conversations with our children. Although Laney's mom used questioning techniques to get the information she needed from her daughter in order to attempt to help reestablish safety, she missed several opportunities to go deeper and model empathy. Furthermore, she didn't manage her own self-awareness adequately enough to stay in the conversation at a deep enough level to meet her child's needs. Rather than restoring safety and making Laney's world manageable, the conversation only taught Laney not to talk to her mom about big, scary things—not the result Laney's mom wanted.

In the following example, a few empathy strategies are incorporated, along with increased emotional awareness, to enable deeper conversations.

Mom: Hi, sweetie. How was school today?

Laney: I don't like school anymore. I don't think I want to go back.

Mom: I'm sorry to hear that. What happened?

Laney: I heard my friends and some of the teachers talking about a school shooting. It scared me. I don't think I should go to school anymore.

Mom: Wow. I can really understand that. Why did the conversation scare you?

Mom validates Laney's feelings and asks additional questions about how she feels. In asking these questions, she is able to help Laney get in touch with her feelings and begin to process what scares her. This is an important step in reconciling her feelings.

Laney: I'm afraid it could happen at our school, too. The teachers think it could happen at our school. I feel like school is becoming a war zone.

Mom: That's a frightening feeling. What did the teachers say about this?

Laney: Well, I heard two of them talking in the library, and they said teachers should be armed. My teacher said I shouldn't worry, but what else am I supposed to think?

Mom: I understand your fear. To be honest, I sometimes worry about schools and safety, too.

Empathy in the World

Laney's mom accomplishes a couple of things here—she acknowledges her daughter's fears and gives voice to her own. In doing this, Mom gives permission for her daughter to be afraid, a normal emotion given the topic. She normalizes the feeling, which takes away the negative stigma and enables both of them to manage the emotions better.

It is important to not get stuck in the fear, however. Let's look at how Mom moves the conversation forward from here:

Laney: You do? You get scared? Why do you let me go to school, then?

Mom: Well, I look at it this way—there are a lot of things to be afraid of in the world nowadays. And I have a choice I have to make about it all: I can be afraid, keep you at home, and keep us all home to try to be safe. Or I can trust that everyone will do the best they can to ensure your safety. For me, I have to trust in the latter. I know the school is aware of the potential dangers, just like I am. And I know that the teachers and staff do everything they can do to keep everyone safe. That is their job. Just like it is my job to keep you as safe as I can. If everyone does their job, that is really all we can do.

Laney: But what if something happens?

Mom: That is a reasonable question. There is also that potential, just like there is always a potential that a natural disaster can happen. Life can feel scary and overwhelming. But I don't want to live in fear all of the time. I have to choose to move past my fear. It is something you will need to learn to choose as well.

Mom is taking the time to explain some very difficult and big feelings to Laney. The type of conversation to have here will really be dependent on the developmental level of the child and the com-

151

fort of the parent to engage in the discussion. My rule of thumb is this: If the child is mature enough to ask the question, he or she is also mature enough to handle the accurate answer, given that the answer is presented in a way that is understandable to the child. This is important. Too often we tend to shortchange answers and miss opportunities for social-emotional growth in an attempt to protect children from difficult feelings. Better to engage in the conversation fully.

Laney: But I'm still afraid. I still don't think I can go to school.

Mom: I understand that. And I think we can figure out how to help you feel safe. But until you are ready to choose for yourself if you want to live in fear, I am here to help you learn to live in spite of your fear. I know it is hard. And there may be days it feels too scary to do. We will have to find ways to work through it. But for now, we are going to work through it together. Deal?

Through honest reflection and a willingness to engage in very difficult, very big conversations, Laney's mom begins the journey of teaching her child how to live in a scary world. To me, this is one of the biggest jobs of a parent. There are many things we can choose to be fearful of, many ways we can limit ourselves because of those fears. Teaching our children how to engage in life even when they have big, scary emotions is a vital aspect of teaching both emotional flexibility and emotional intelligence.

Let's see how the conversation ends.

Laney: Do you promise I will be safe?

Mom: I promise the school, Daddy, and I will do everything we can to keep you safe.

Laney: Okay. I can try to go back tomorrow.

Mom: That sounds good. What can I do to help you feel safe?

Mom makes no promises that aren't truthful, no guarantees about things beyond her control. This level of honesty creates an internal safety. Laney instinctively knows she can trust what her mother is saying because it feels truthful. Furthermore, Mom has created the potential for further conversations about difficult subjects by her responses here.

At this point, Laney and her mom will continue to discuss ways to feel safe at school and how to manage her emotions. An important foundation has been built.

Acts of Injustice

One of the earliest names for Generation Z wasn't iGen; it was Plurals. This name was given because, as I mentioned in Chapter 1, iGen is perhaps the generation most tolerant of diversity to date (Twenge, 2017). This tolerance can create discomfort as children recognize the intolerances and acts of injustice that abound throughout the world. Acts of terrorism against specific groups of people, racism, sexism, ageism—all of these feel ever-present in the world and are creating increased levels of distress in our children.

In the following scenario, a middle school aged child has witnessed an act of bullying against a classmate related to gender identification. Distraught, she seeks advice from her parents.

Scenario

Maddie was born male. Despite her biology, she has never really identified as male, only female. To her friends, she is a girl. To her parents, she is a girl. But to some who don't understand gender identity differences, she is something else. School is often difficult for Maddie because of her gender identity differences. This has been particularly true this year, in seventh grade.

The Caring Child

One day, Khari, a friend of Maddie's since second grade, witnessed two eighth graders picking on Maddie. They taunted Maddie and called her names. Everywhere she tried to go to on campus, the two eighth graders were there. Khari told Maddie to tell her teacher, the counselor, the administration—someone. But this was hard for Maddie.

Day after day, the taunting continued. Day after day, Maddie stayed silent. Finally, Khari stood up and told the principal about the problems Maddie was having with the eighth graders. Maddie was called into the counselor's office. The eighth graders were called into the administrator's office. They were all mad at Khari for saying anything to anyone.

Initial Dialogue

In this scenario, Khari goes home after being yelled at by Maddie and threatened by the two eighth graders. She is confused and upset about her friend's response to her and the incident in general. Watch as her mother tries to help Khari understand what has happened and how to move forward:

Mom: How was school today?

Khari: Horrible.

Mom: What happened?

Khari: Two kids have been bullying Maddie because she is a "she" now. So, I told Principal Newman about it. Maddie had to go up to the office. So did the boys. After school, Maddie got mad at me and said I was a bad friend. The boys got mad, too, although I don't care what they said. I just don't know why Maddie is mad at me. And I don't understand why the boys had to be so mean to her just because she likes to be called "she" now. What's it to them? She isn't hurting them. It's not like she's into them.

Mom: Maddie got mad when you told the principal about the bullying?

Khari: Yeah.

Mom: I'm sorry. I think you did the right thing. I'm sure she will be fine in a day or two.

Khari: She said she didn't want to be my friend anymore, that I didn't understand what she was going through. Do you think she's right?

Mom: I think you should always speak out for what's right, and bullying is just wrong.

Khari: I think so, too. But I don't want Maddie to be mad at me.

Mom: Like I said, I'm sure she'll get past it. Just give her a few days. Now, what do you want for dinner?

Analysis of Dialogue

In this example, Khari is wrestling with the difficulties of changing societal norms and the potential impact of being an upstander. Mom does a nice job trying to support her daughter. However, she doesn't go deep enough into the situation to help her daughter understand what is happening. Nor does she broach the subject of gender identity at all, despite her daughter's wonderings. These two missed opportunities prevent deeper learning from happening.

Let's examine the dialogue closely to see where a different response could have helped Khari understand both Maddie's response and the larger gender issues.

Mom: How was school today?

Khari: Horrible.

Mom: What happened?

The Caring Child

> *Khari:* Two kids have been bullying Maddie because she is a "she" now. So, I told Principal Newman about it. Maddie had to go up to the office. So did the boys. After school, Maddie got mad at me and said I was a bad friend. The boys got mad, too, although I don't care what they said. I just don't know why Maddie is mad at me. And I don't understand why the boys had to be so mean to her just because she likes to be called "she" now. What's it to them? She isn't hurting them. It's not like she's into them.

This is a good start to the conversation. Khari is open and demonstrates readiness to have a full conversation about the situation.

> *Mom:* Maddie got mad when you told the principal about the bullying?
>
> *Khari:* Yeah.
>
> *Mom:* I'm sorry. I think you did the right thing. I'm sure she will be fine in a day or two.

Although Mom validates Khari's actions, her response makes it clear that she is not interested in a deep discussion on the many issues raised by Khari's description of the event.

> *Khari:* She said she didn't want to be my friend anymore, that I didn't understand what she was going through. Do you think she's right?
>
> *Mom:* I think you should always speak out for what's right, and bullying is just wrong.
>
> *Khari:* I think so, too. But I don't want Maddie to be mad at me.
>
> *Mom:* Like I said, I'm sure she'll get past it. Just give her a few days. Now, what do you want for dinner?

Empathy in the World

Mom cuts the conversation short. She doesn't make use of the opportunities to answer the many questions Khari has.

New Dialogue Using Coaching Strategies

As mentioned earlier, the short conversation above is not horrible. It just doesn't afford opportunities for deep discussions about the difficult issues Khari raises. By missing these teachable moments, Khari doesn't get an opportunity to practice social awareness skills, deepen empathy and compassion, and broaden her understanding of the world.

In the revised dialogue, Mom uses a few strategies to enter into the conversation in a deeper way.

Mom: How was school today?

Khari: Horrible.

Mom: I'm sorry to hear that. Would you like to talk about what happened?

In this example, Mom demonstrates compassion for Khari's feelings and invites a deeper conversation. The difference is subtle, but it conveys deeper meaning that will shape the rest of the conversation.

Khari: Well, two kids have been bullying Maddie all year because she is a "she" now. I told Principal Newman about it. Maddie had to go up to the office. So did the boys. After school, Maddie got mad at me and said I was a bad friend. The boys got mad, too, although I don't care what they said. I just don't know why Maddie is mad at me. And I don't understand why the boys had to be so mean to her just because she likes to be called "she" now. What's it to them? She isn't hurting them. It's not like she's into them.

157

The Caring Child

Mom:	It sounds like a very hard day. Very upsetting.

Mom demonstrates empathy in this response.

Khari:	It was. I just don't understand why Maddie got so mad.
Mom:	I'm sorry. Did you talk to her about the bullying before you went to the principal?
Khari:	She told me not to do anything. But after watching the boys be such jerks and seeing Maddie cry, I couldn't do nothing.
Mom:	I understand that. How do you think Maddie felt when you told the principal after she asked you not to?

Mom is beginning to ask questions that can help Khari see the impact of her actions and understand Maddie's perspective a bit more.

Khari:	Are you saying I shouldn't have said anything?
Mom:	No, not necessarily. It is important to speak out against injustice and in favor of people who don't have a voice. But, even though you did something good, there can be unforeseen consequences. Sometimes people are too afraid to speak up. Sometimes people don't want help.
Khari:	Does that mean we shouldn't help?
Mom:	Not always. But it does mean that we need to consider others' feelings, too.

Mom is taking the time to explain the difficult concepts of unforeseen consequences and the impact of one's actions. Exploring these concepts will help Khari deepen both her social awareness and her empathy skills.

Khari: But how do I know when I should do what my friend wants versus doing what I think is the right thing to do?

Mom: That's a good question. What do you think you should do?

From here, Khari's mom can coach her on how to find ways to follow her ethics, help those who don't have a voice, and empathize when her friends struggle with her decision to get involved. This conversation also lends itself to answering another one of Khari's big questions—why do people marginalize and bully others? These are difficult conversations, but important ones. By demonstrating a willingness to enter into complicated and often confusing discussions about large events and feelings, the parent has an opportunity to demonstrate empathy and compassion, as well as model ways to use emotional intelligence every day. Tip Sheet 22: Talking About the Hard Stuff may give you a place to start.

TIP SHEET 22
Talking About the Hard Stuff

» Focus on your relationships with your children—first, foremost, always.

» Create a safe and trusting environment.

» Communicate your values.

» Be open and honest.

» Don't shy away from difficulty questions—lean in.

» If your child asks, give him or her an answer that is developmentally appropriate.

» Speak facts, not fear.

» Listen to your child.

Note. Adapted from Fonseca, 2016.

It's a Stress-Filled World

No conversation about empathy and the world would be complete without a discussion of overwhelm. The world has become louder. The 24-hour news cycle bombards our senses every moment of every day. Tech and social media addiction, as well as the never-ending auditory and visual onslaught, have created increased anxious-like behaviors in children and adults. As discussed in Chapter 1, the statistics on iGen make it clear that anxiety and depression are on the rise (Twenge, 2017). I suspect this will be true for future generations as well. Why wouldn't it? The noise hasn't change. The constant cycle of media hasn't diminished. The lack of balance in our digital lives hasn't yet lessened. Stress and anxiety in toxic levels, it appears, are here to stay.

In the following scenario, a high-performing high school student wrestles with overwhelm caused not only by her highly scheduled life and dreams of college, but also by the information overload ever present in her digital world.

Scenario

Liana is a senior at a top-performing high school. She lives with her aunt and three cousins. Her parents were deported 18 months ago, and, aside from phone calls weekly, she has limited contact with them.

Liana is experiencing significant levels of stress. Although she tries to hide the impact of her stress and anxiety on her daily functioning from her aunt, her overwhelm builds to the point of impacting her ability to get her school work done and function at home and at school.

Empathy in the World

Initial Dialogue

In this scenario, Liana's aunt, Marianna, confronts Liana about her anxious behavior and obvious high levels of stress.

Aunt Marianna:	Liana, I need to speak with you. I am worried about you. You are struggling with your work, you seem tired all of the time, and you seem to be angry or sad a lot. What is going on with you? Have you taken on too many things lately?
Liana:	It's nothing, Tía. Really.
Aunt Marianna:	You know you can talk to me about anything, right? So again, what's up? Is it your parents? Are you missing them?
Liana:	Always. But I'm fine. I've just been really busy.
Aunt Marianna:	I knew you took too much on this semester. Maybe you need to take a break, pull back a little.
Liana:	I can't. I need all of this stuff for my college applications. I'm fine. Really.
Aunt Marianna:	You're not fine. I remember when I was in high school. Things felt so overwhelming to me. I had to learn that I needed to balance my life. Trust me, you don't need to make yourself crazy to get into school. If you just pull back a little—
Liana:	Tía, stop. You don't understand what it's like now. Things are different than when you went to high school.
Aunt Marianna:	Not that different. You need to trust me. You need more balance.

Liana:	That's not it. And I'm fine.
Aunt Marianna:	You're stubborn, just like your father. He had to learn about balance, too.
Liana:	I appreciate what you are doing, Tía. But, honestly, this conversation is creating more stress right now. I've got homework to do, okay? I promise things are fine. If that changes, I'll reach out to you, okay? Trust me.
Aunt Marianna:	Okay, mija. I just worry about you. You're too hard on yourself, try to do too much.
Liana:	Like I said, I'm fine. Love you. *(She gets up and leaves.)*

Analysis of Dialogue

In this scenario, Aunt Marianna is trying to initiate a difficult conversation with Liana. Although she asks several questions and makes several attempts during the conversation, Liana is uninterested in speaking with her aunt about her feelings. When her aunt attempts to use personal examples, the conversation becomes even more blocked. In the end, Liana doesn't discuss her feelings, nor is there evidence that she will open up about her anxious-behaviors with her aunt in the future.

Let's examine the conversation closer to see if there are missed opportunities to connect with Liana and engage her in an honest conversation about her feelings:

Aunt Marianna:	Liana, I need to speak with you. I am worried about you. You are struggling with your work, you seem tired all of the time, and you seem to be angry or sad a lot. What is

going on with you? Have you taken on too many things lately?

Liana: It's nothing, Tía. Really.

Immediately in the conversation, Aunt Marianna uses words that will put Liana on the defensive. This type of conversation initiation usually creates more roadblocks than opportunities.

Aunt Marianna: You know you can talk to me about anything, right? So again, what's up? Is it your parents? Are you missing them?

Liana: Always. But I'm fine. I've just been really busy.

Aunt Marianna: I knew you took too much on this semester. Maybe you need to take a break, pull back a little.

Aunt Marianna continues to try to start the conversation with Liana. However, the roadblocks and difficulties of the topic prevent Liana from engaging. In the end, Aunt Marianna's assumptions about the problem further close off the possibility for open communication.

Liana: I can't. I need all of this stuff for my college applications. I'm fine. Really.

Aunt Marianna: You're not fine. I remember when I was in high school. Things felt so overwhelming to me. I had to learn that I needed to balance my life. Trust me, you don't need to make yourself crazy to get into school. If you just pull back a little—

Liana: Tía, stop. You don't understand what it's like now. Things are different than when you went to high school.

The Caring Child

In this part of the dialogue, Liana begins to give signs of her overwhelm. However, the opportunity to probe further is missed as Aunt Marianna instead shifts the conversation to personal examples, negating opportunities for engagement about Liana and Liana's feelings or needs.

Aunt
Marianna: Not that different. You need to trust me. You need more balance.

Liana: That's not it. And I'm fine.

Aunt
Marianna: You're stubborn, just like your father. He had to learn about balance, too.

The conversation has gone from the potential for open dialogue to more of a lecture. This presents another barrier and further reduces the change of future conversations.

Liana: I appreciate what you are doing, Tía. But, honestly, this conversation is creating more stress right now. I've got homework to do, okay? I promise things are fine. If that changes, I'll reach out to you, okay? Trust me.

Aunt
Marianna: Okay, mija. I just worry about you. You're too hard on yourself, try to do too much.

Liana: Like I said, I'm fine. Love you. *(She gets up and leaves.)*

At this point, the conversation is over. Liana, although respectful and appreciative of her aunt, is not going to talk about her feelings or express her needs. Opportunities to address the concerns that Aunt Marianna has are gone, and it is unlikely that future conversations will yield different results.

New Dialogue Using Coaching Strategies

Using different strategies focused on relationships and empathy, different outcomes can be achieved in this conversation. Let's look at alternative ways to guide the conversation with Liana:

Aunt Marianna:	Hi, Liana. How was your day? It seems like you have been very busy lately.
Liana:	Today was fine. I'm just really busy.
Aunt Marianna:	I get that. Senior year is so busy. College apps, school, activities, thoughts about the future . . . it can be overwhelming.

Aunt Marianna starts off with a neutral entry into a conversation, enabling a less triggering discussion. This sets the stage for the deeper questions Aunt Marianna wants to ask and prevents a defensive response from Liana.

Liana:	Always. It is, definitely. Nothing I can't handle, though.
Aunt Marianna:	Ha. You sound like your father. He always wanted to make sure people thought he could handle anything. It's hard having them gone.
Liana:	Yep.

Aunt Marianna acknowledges some feelings Liana likely has, while beginning to set in motion some other discussions in which she wants to engage.

Aunt Marianna:	How have you been feeling about everything? We haven't really had a chance to talk lately.
Liana:	It's hard. I really miss them. Sometimes I worry I'll never see them again.
Aunt Marianna:	I understand that. I imagine it's a pretty scary feeling. And really sad.

By talking about the deeper issues in this way, it is easier to talk about the overwhelm as a whole. Aunt Marianna makes the conversation easy; there is no need for defensive responses.

Liana:	Yeah. And I don't want them to worry about me, so I can't really tell them about that.
Aunt Marianna:	Do you feel like you have to just keep it all inside?
Liana:	Sometimes, yeah.
Aunt Marianna:	That must be hard. Overwhelming.
Liana:	It really is.

Using reflection and empathy, Aunt Marianna is able to show empathy and compassion for the difficulties Liana may be having, without making Liana feel like she is broken in some way. This normalizes her emotions and makes them easier to discuss.

Aunt Marianna:	Is there anything I can do to help? Anything you need from me?

Empathy in the World

Liana:	Just understanding. I know I've been off lately. I'm just so overwhelmed. Between school, my parents, college, worrying about the future. Some days I can't cope. I just want to scream or cry.
Aunt Marianna:	That makes sense to me! I think I might feel the same way in your shoes. You can always cry here, you know. I might even cry with you!
Liana:	*(Laughs)* Thanks. I appreciate you. It's hard for me, though—to be open like that.
Aunt Marianna:	Why?
Liana:	I feel too exposed, you know?
Aunt Marianna:	Yeah, I get it. You are safe with me, mija. You can be whoever or whatever you need to be with me. Okay?
Liana:	Thanks.

Aunt Marianna does a great job creating the space Liana needs to talk about her overwhelm openly. Aunt Marianna offers empathy, compassion, and even some advice. Liana is in a position to hear and accept the support being offered. This happens because of the empathetic response without Aunt Marianna changing the focus.

At this point, Aunt Marianna is in a good position to have future conversations with Liana. Each time they are able to talk openly about difficult subjects, it creates the space for future discussions and builds on the positive relationship formed between the two participants.

Life is filled with stressful events—some big and some small. Talking openly with children about their stress and giving them strategies to beat back the overwhelm are critical for children. Tip Sheet 23: Teaching Children to R.O.A.R. features my method for working through overwhelm. It has helped hundreds of people—children and adults—in my practice. It'll help you and your children, too!

TIP SHEET 23
Teaching Children to R.O.A.R.

Breaking free of stress and overwhelm may seem daunting, but it needn't be. R.O.A.R.—or *Relax, Orient, Attune, and Release*—is an efficient way to regain a sense of calm when things become too much. Use this with your kids at home, and teach them to use it anywhere.

- » **R = RELAX:** Start by relaxing your body and brain. Take a deep breath and practice a mindful moment.

- » **O = ORIENT:** Shift your attention to the present moment—only the present moment.

- » **A = ATTUNE:** Focus on your needs right now. What do you need in this moment? How can that need be met?

- » **R = RELEASE:** Lean into your feelings. Let go of the hold of the stress and anxiety. Give up any resistance and trust that you are okay.

It may take a little time for R.O.A.R to become a habit. But the more you practice the skills, the sooner it will feel natural.

This chapter examined just a few of the larger issues confronting our children, with role-plays to highlight how our conversations can help our children mature their empathy and compassion responses. The more you can practice modeling empathy for your children, the better. The more your conversations nurture their emotional intelligence and resilience, the more your children are prepared to enter the world.

One of the biggest take-away messages from Twenge's (2017) book *iGen* is how unprepared our children are to enter adulthood. Delving into deep conversations that give children opportunities to practice emotional and cognitive flexibility is one way to bridge the gap and help our children step into adulthood ready to handle whatever life has in store.

Cultivating Caring Action Steps

The final chapter of *The Caring Child* focused on role-plays related to big feelings around the concepts of injustice, bullying, and trauma. Learning to be vulnerable with children, have appropriate conversations on very difficult topics, and empower our children to take action on the things they are passionate about can be very difficult. Oftentimes, we, as parents, are afraid of going too deep too fast or engaging in complicated discussion too early. It is important to allow your children to guide you in this area. They will indicate their readiness for conversations. Your job is to be open to having the conversation when they are ready, engaging in deeper and deeper ways. The action steps in this chapter involve using service projects as a way to connect empathy to the world as a whole. Through service projects, families can explore deep issues together, while also modeling compassion and empathy.

1. Make a list with your family members of a variety of service projects for family involvement. This can include things like working in a community pantry; organizing a drive to send letters to our troops on deployment; being part of a community event for local lesbian, gay, bisexual, transgender, and queer (LGBTQ) youth; or coordinating a book drive for communities impacted by natural disasters.

2. Once you've created a list, pick one to three events to be involved with throughout the year. Discuss why the service activity is important to the family, and how it relates to family expectations and individual character strengths.

3. Create a plan for involvement that ensures that all family members contribute to the service activity. Remember to debrief about the activity after completion, taking time to connect it back to empathy and compassion.

Final Thoughts

THE world can often feel like a big and scary place—a place where it is easy to feel disconnected and isolated, despite the ability to hop on your smartphones and snap a friend. Today's children are the most tech-connected to the world, the most tolerant of the differences between human beings, and the most willing to hear each other's stories compared to previous generations. They are also the most isolated, most afraid, and least resilient. The results of this dichotomy are challenges with developing emotional intelligence, stress resilience, and the connection between empathy, compassion, and reasoning. Fortunately, it isn't too late to overcome these challenges and create a more caring world.

I hope that the information contained on these pages gives you the information, strategies, and resources you need to overcome today's challenges. I believe our children are our most precious world resource. If we can support their natural caring nature, teach them to be emotionally flexible and resilient, and support them as they try to create a more compassionate world, then we will have done our part to leave the planet at least a little better than we've departed from it.

The Caring Child

The work I've outlined here may sound easy. It may even sound simplistic and or redundant. In truth, it is not. Developing our emotional intelligence can be challenging. Our children will go through periods of resistance. We will wonder if we've made things worse, hindered our children's development in some ways. When you feel this way—and you will if you are engaged with your children at all—you must remember that you are doing the best you can in the moment. Sometimes that will be a great example of parenting or teaching. Sometimes not. But regardless, keep showing up. Develop your emotional intelligence skills. Be an example of empathy and compassion. Practice emotional flexibility. Model what you want to see in your children.

In the end, it doesn't matter how often we fail to meet our expectations or how often we have to apologize and try again. It matters that we are still present, still trying, still developing. That is what our children will remember. That is what will give them permission to be "works in progress," forever growing their emotional intelligence, forever enhancing their empathy and compassion.

I love hearing about how my work has impacted you and your family. Please feel free to contact me with your personal stories of triumph, your struggles and challenges, and what strategies have worked best for you. Reach me via e-mail at christine@christine fonseca.com or on my many social networking sites. Together we can help our children embrace a balanced approach to emotional intelligence, one that encompasses both the heart and the head, and one that celebrates emotional flexibility and reasoned responses.

References

American Academy of Pediatrics. (2016). *American Academy of Pediatrics announces new recommendations for children's media use*. Retrieved from https://www.aap.org/en-us/about-the-aap/aap-press-room/Pages/American-Academy-of-Pediatrics-Announces-New-Recommendations-for-Childrens-Media-Use.aspx

Anderson, M., & Jiang, J. (2018). Teens, social media & technology 2018. *Pew Research Center*. Retrieved from https://www.pewinternet.org/2018/05/31/teens-social-media-technology-2018

Babic, M. J., Smith, J. J., Morgan, P. J., Eather, N., Plotnikoff, R. C., & Lubans, D. R. (2017). Longitudinal associations between changes in screen-time and mental health outcomes in adolescents. *Mental Health and Physical Activity, 12,* 124–131. doi:10.1016/j.mhpa.2017.04.001

Bamber, M. D., & Schneider, J. K. (2016). Mindfulness-based meditation to decrease stress and anxiety in college students: A narrative synthesis of the research. *Educational Research Review, 18,* 1–32.

Baron-Cohen, S. (2011). *The science of evil: On empathy and the origins of cruelty*. New York, NY: Basic Books.

Bloom, P. (2016). *Against empathy: The case for rational compassion*. New York, NY: Ecco.

Center for Promise. (2018). *Disciplined and disconnected: The experience of exclusionary discipline in Minnesota and the promise of non-exclusionary alternatives*. Retrieved from https://gradnation. americaspromise.org/report/disciplined-and-disconnected

de Waal, F. B. (2009). Putting the altruism back into altruism: The evolution of empathy. *Annual Review of Psychology, 59*, 279–300. doi:10.1146/annurev.psych.59.103006.093625

Decety, J., & Jackson, P. L. (2004). The functional architecture of human empathy. *Behavioral and Cognitive Neuroscience Reviews, 3*, 71–100. doi:10.1177/2F1534582304267187

Decety, J., Norman, G. J., Berntson, G. G., & Cacioppo, J. T. (2012). A neurobehavioral evolutionary perspective on the mechanisms underlying empathy. *Progress in Neurobiology, 98*, 38–48.

Durlak, J. A., Weissberg, R. P., Dymnicki, A. B., Taylor, R. D., & Schellinger, K. B. (2011). The impact of enhancing students' social and emotional learning: A meta-analysis of school-based universal interventions. *Child Development, 82*, 405–432.

Fonseca, C. (2015). *I'm not just gifted: Social-emotional curriculum for guiding gifted children*. Waco, TX: Prufrock Press.

Fonseca, C. (2016). *Emotional intensity in gifted students: Helping kids cope with explosive feelings* (2nd ed.). Waco, TX: Prufrock Press.

Fonseca, C. (2017). *Letting go: A girl's guide to breaking free of stress and anxiety*. Waco, TX: Prufrock Press.

Fonseca, C. (2020). *Healing the heart: Helping your child thrive after trauma*. Waco, TX: Prufrock Press. Manuscript in preparation.

Gilbert, P. (2010). Compassion focused therapy. In W. Dryden (Series Ed.), *The CBT distinctive features series*. New York, NY: Routledge.

Gilbert, P., & Procter, S. (2006). Compassionate mind training for people with high shame and self-criticism: overview and pilot study of a group therapy approach. *Clinical Psychology and Psychotherapy, 13*, 353–379. doi:10.1002/cpp.507

References

Goetz, J. L., Keltner, D., & Simon-Thomas, E. (2010). Compassion: An evolutionary analysis and empirical review. *Psychological Bulletin, 136,* 351–374.

Graham, L. (2013). *Bouncing back: Rewiring your brain for maximum resilience and well-being.* Novato, CA: New World Library.

Graham, L. (2018). *Resilience and the brain.* Poster session presented at The Art and Science of Connecting Mind, Body, and Emotion for Student Success Conference, Scotts Valley, CA.

Hotwire. (2018). *Understanding generation alpha.* Retrieved from https://www.hotwireglobal.com/feature/understanding-generation-alpha-2

Jones, S., Brush, K., Bailey, R., Brion-Meisels, G., McIntyre, J., Kahn, J., . . . Stickle, L. (2017). *Navigating SEL from the inside out: Looking inside and across 25 leading SEL programs.* Cambridge, MA: Harvard Graduate School of Education.

McGonigal, K. (2015). *The upside of stress: Why stress is good for you, and how to get good at it.* New York, NY: Avery.

Neff, K. (2003a). Self-compassion: An alternative conceptualization of a healthy attitude toward oneself. *Self and Identity, 2,* 85–101.

Neff, K. (2003b). The development and validation of a scale to measure self-compassion. *Self and Identity, 2,* 223–250.

Niemiec R. M. (2013). VIA character strengths: Research and practice (The first 10 years). In H. Knoop & A. Delle Fave (Eds.), *Well-being and cultures: Perspectives from positive psychology* (Vol. 3, pp. 11–29). Dordrecht, Netherlands: Springer.

Odgers, C. (2018). Smartphones are bad for some teens, not all. *Nature, 554,* 432–434. doi:10.1038/d41586-018-02109-8

Przybylski, A. K., & Weinstein, N. (2019). Digital screen time limits and young children's psychological well-being: Evidence from a population based study. *Child Development, 90,* e56–e65. https://doi.org/10.1111/cdev.13007

Saufler, C. (2011). *School climate, the brain and connection to school.* Retrieved from https://www.iirp.edu/pdf/Bethlehem-2012-Presentations/Bethlehem-2012-Saufler.pdf

Singer, T., & Klimecki, O. M. (2014). Empathy and compassion. *Current Biology, 18,* R875–R878.

Singer, T., & Lamm, C. (2009). The social neuroscience of empathy. *Annals of the New York Academy of Sciences, 1156,* 81–96.

Stafford, C. (2018). *Stress, sleep, cell-phones, and smarts: The neuroscience behind teenage motivation and performance.* Poster session presented at the American Counseling Association Annual Conference: Reach for the Stars, Los Angeles, CA.

Stevens, L., & Woodruff, C. C. (Eds.). (2018). *The neuroscience of empathy, compassion, and self-compassion.* London, England: Academic Press.

Stiglic, N., & Viner, R. M. (2019). Effects of screentime on health and well-being of children and adolescents: A systematic review of reviews. *BMJ Open, 9*(e023191). doi:10.1136/bmjopen-2018-023191

Straker, L., Zabatiero, J., Danby, S., Thorpe, K., & Edwards, S. (2019). Conflicting guidelines on young children's screen time and use of digital technology create policy and practice dilemmas. *The Journal of Pediatrics, 202,* 300–303. doi:10.1016/j.peds.2018.07.019

Twenge, J. M. (2017). *iGen: Why today's super-connected kids are growing up less rebellious, more tolerant, less happy—and completely unprepared for adulthood.* New York, NY: Atria Books.

Twenge, J. M. (2019). The sad state of happiness in the United States and the role of digital media. *World Happiness Report.* Retrieved from https://worldhappiness.report/ed/2019/the-sad-state-of-happiness-in-the-united-states-and-the-role-of-digital-media

Twenge, J. M., & Campbell, W. K. (2018). Associations between screen time and lower psychological well-being among children and adolescents: Evidence from a population-based study. *Preventive Medicine Reports, 12,* 271–283. doi:10.1016/j.pmedr.2018.10.003.

Twenge, J. M., Joiner, T. E., Rogers, M. I., & Martin, G. N. (2018). Increases in depressive symptoms, suicide-related outcomes, and suicide rates among U.S. adolescents after 2010 and links to

References

increased new media screen time. *Clinical Psychological Science, 6,* 3–17. https://doi.org/10.1177/2167702617723376

Wang, S. (2005). A conceptual framework for integrating research related to the physiology of compassion and the wisdom of Buddhist teachers. In P. Gilbert (Ed.), *Compassion: Conceptualisations, research, and the use in psychotherapy* (pp. 75–120). New York, NY: Routledge.

Willis, J. (2018). *How emotion impacts the brain's successful learning and what to do about it.* Poster session presented at The Art and Science of Connecting Mind, Body, and Emotion for Student Success Conference, Scotts Valley, CA.

Zink, J., Belcher, B. R., Kechter, A., Stone, M. D., & Leventhal, A. M. (2019). Reciprocal associations between screen time and emotional disorders symptoms during adolescence. *Preventive Medicine Reports, 13,* 281–288. doi:10.1016/jmedr.2019.01.014

About the Author

Christine Fonseca is a licensed educational psychologist, critically acclaimed author of fiction and nonfiction, and a nationally recognized speaker on topics related to educational psychology, mental health, and giftedness. Drawing on her expertise as a psychologist and parenting coach, Christine contributes to *Psychology Today*, authoring the parenting blog Parenting for a New Generation. She has written self-help articles for Parents.com, Johnson & Johnson, and *Justine Magazine*. Her critically acclaimed titles include *Emotional Intensity in Gifted Students*, *Raising the Shy Child*, and *Letting Go: A Girl's Guide to Breaking Free of Stress and Anxiety*.

Christine lives in Southern California with her husband and children. When she isn't crafting new books, she can be found with her head deep in a book, sipping too many iced teas at the local coffee house with friends, or roaming a local beach with her family. For more information about Christine or her books, visit her website https://christinefonseca.com or find her on social media.

For Product Safety Concerns and Information please contact our EU
representative GPSR@taylorandfrancis.com
Taylor & Francis Verlag GmbH, Kaufingerstraße 24, 80331 München, Germany

www.ingramcontent.com/pod-product-compliance
Ingram Content Group UK Ltd.
Pitfield, Milton Keynes, MK11 3LW, UK
UKHW021432080625
459435UK00011B/246